# The Stay Interview

## A Manager's Guide to Keeping the Best and Brightest

### RICHARD P. FINNEGAN

 **AMACOM** AMERICAN MANAGEMENT ASSOCIATION

New York ▸ Atlanta ▸ Brussels ▸ Chicago ▸ Mexico City ▸ San Francisco
Shanghai ▸ Tokyo ▸ Toronto ▸ Washington, D.C.

Bulk discounts available. For details visit: www.amacombooks.org/go/specialsales
Or contact special sales:
Phone: 800-250-5308 / Email: specialsls@amanet.org
View all the AMACOM titles at: www.amacombooks.org
American Management Association: www.amanet.org

This publication is designed to provide accurate and authoritative information in regard to the subject matter covered. It is sold with the understanding that the publisher is not engaged in rendering legal, accounting, or other professional service. If legal advice or other expert assistance is required, the services of a competent professional person should be sought.

Library of Congress Cataloging-in-Publication Data
Finnegan, Richard P.
The stay interview : a manager's guide to keeping the best and brightest / Richard P. Finnegan.
     pages cm
Includes index.
ISBN 978-0-8144-3649-3 (pbk.) — ISBN 978-0-8144-3650-9 (ebook)
1. Employee attitude surveys. 2. Employee retention. I. Title.
HF5549.5.A83F568 2015
658.3'14—dc23
                                        2014045749

**About AMA**

American Management Association (www.amanet.org) is a world leader in talent development, advancing the skills of individuals to drive business success. Our mission is to support the goals of individuals and organizations through a complete range of products and services, including classroom and virtual seminars, webcasts, webinars, podcasts, conferences, corporate and government solutions, business books, and research. AMA's approach to improving performance combines experiential learning—learning through doing—with opportunities for ongoing professional growth at every step of one's career journey.

Printing number
10 9 8 7 6 5 4 3 2 1

# CONTENTS

# The Stay Interview

he concept of stay interviews seems way too simple. Is it really possible to improve your team's engagement, retention, and productivity just by asking employees what you can do to make their jobs better?

The answer is "yes" because stay interviews address the two great crises facing business today simply, cheaply, and where the crises originate.

According to the Bureau of Labor Statistics, the number of employees who voluntarily quit is increasing sharply each year,[1] while Gallup finds that since 2000 employee engagement levels in the United States have hardly budged, and they were dismal to start. Seventy percent of American workers are not engaged by their jobs, and 18 percent are actively disengaged. Only 30 percent are engaged, which means that more than twice as many people are committed to avoiding their work as there are committed to doing it.[2]

To combat these disastrous trends we will soon be spending, according to a third study, $1.5 billion each year on top of the other billions we have already spent.[3] These dollars are poured into well-intentioned initiatives such as Career Day, Employee Appreciation Week, town hall meetings, better newsletters—all the scattershot, impersonal things that corporate imagines will make companies better.

However, when was the last time you heard a really good worker say, "My boss treats me like dirt, but I'm holding on for Employee Appreciation Week. I'll get a balloon and a hot dog and I'll be stoked for another year"?

The trouble with these programs is that they are implemented *above and around each employee's direct supervisor*, and the data has long been clear and conclusive: The primary reason employees work harder and stay longer is a good relationship with their direct supervisors.

As one-on-one meetings between leaders and both newly hired and continuing employees, stay interviews reinforce good relationships, forge new ones, and help repair those that are strained. On that small foundation great companies are built.

## What Are Stay Interviews?

To know what stay interviews are, it is important to note what they are *not*.

- They are not team meetings or focus groups. They are private, individual meetings with each employee.

- They are not conducted by HR because supervisors are "too busy." They are conducted by direct supervisors, who must own their talent.

- They are not intended to craft development plans. They aren't based on the assumption that all employees want to grow. And they don't prioritize professional growth over schedules, colleagues, input, and other aspects of work. They reveal what is important to the employees and how their desires can be satisfied.

‣ They are not focused on job performance. They are aimed instead at making employees' work lives more rewarding and comfortable.

‣ They are not something faddish to be done occasionally. They are a management priority conducted on a specific schedule with required follow-ups.

Consider the processes your company employs to help you manage your team. Do these processes actually improve engagement, retention, and productivity or do they simply clutter your relationships? Do they provide the most direct way to identify and solve productivity obstacles? Do they consider your employees' points of view? Think about:

‣ *Performance reviews*, during which employees wonder if they're being treated fairly and managers dread giving uncomfortable feedback

‣ *Engagement surveys*, from which we get scores for our teams, assume they all think the same way, then guess at the correct solutions

‣ *Exit surveys*, from which we learn how we could have kept an employee, based on the assumption that the employee has told the truth

> *Management training classes,* the so-called soft skills training, where techniques seem easy to apply until we slide back into the reality of our jobs and working with real people

> *Rounding,* or management-by-walking-about, which is based on the idea that superficial, "How's it going?" chitchat will inspire the troops

These processes might get you some insights into the source of problems you can act on before it's too late, but that's not what they're designed to do. Stay interviews, on the other hand, will enable you to get at problems immediately, surgically, and comprehensively.

## What's in It for You?

It is easy to argue that by implementing stay interviews your organization will perform better, your executives will shine, and your board will be pleased. The best reason for implementing them, though, is for your own happiness both now and for the rest of your career. Let's be selfish for a minute and think about the benefits of stay interviews to you as a manager:

> You are accountable for producing work that is measured in numbers that you must achieve.

> Your main method to achieve these numbers is to get more productive work from your team.

> Your achieving these numbers consistently, year after year, puts you in position to retain your job and get promoted to a higher job.

▸ Your achieving these numbers consistently also positions you for even better jobs with other companies.

▸ Your failing to achieve these numbers, though, reduces your chances for better jobs and increases your chances of losing your job.

▸ And besides, winning at work makes you happy. Gallup has begun a survey of the world that will last one hundred years in order to learn what makes people happy, and the leader after the first six years is "a good job."[4]

▸ Work happiness leads to life happiness, too, whether in the form of better relationships, better vacations, or just knowing your life is stable.

Stay interviews don't just make more satisfied employees. They make more satisfied managers, too.

## What Traits Do Stay Interviewers Require?

Just one: trust. Organizational psychologists have dug deep into the reasons why employees perform better and stay longer, and they've found that you win because they trust you. Think of peer managers in your company who build trust with their teams versus those who do not; what good behaviors do the former have as a result, and what poor behaviors do the latter have? Or contrast the best boss you've worked for and the worst. It's a sure bet that you trusted the best and not the worst, which enabled you to accept the shortcomings of the best while you were blinded to the strengths of the worst.

Stay interviews are the ticket to trust-building because they are delivered from the heart. Asking employees how you can make their jobs better comes with no strings. You are not there to talk about their job performance or what happened last week but instead to talk about *them*. How inspired would you be if your boss said: "I cannot do everything but I will do whatever I can . . . and I will stretch my creativity and push upstream if necessary to support any smart, useful idea if it makes you more engaged in your work and you stay here longer."

Even saying "No, I can't" during a stay interview builds trust because you've listened to, considered, and weighed every alternative before delivering that news.

The benefits of trust to a company are easily measurable. *Fortune's* list of *The Top 100 Companies to Work For* is published each February, and the best companies are touted for their wellness centers, strong benefits, and other perks. The fine print, though, reveals that the rankings are weighted mostly by how much employees trust their managers. Not surprisingly, the publicly traded companies on this list see their stock prices grow threefold higher than the stocks of companies not on the list. Trust leads to profits.[5]

## What Stands in My Way?

Time. I've coached thousands of managers to conduct stay interviews and the single difference between success and failure is whether those managers invested the time to conduct stay interviews effectively.

Those who win with stay interviews schedule them on time and build the best possible stay plans they can. Those who are fated to lose say something like:

▸ "You just don't know how many meetings I have and the deadlines on my plate."

‣ "We have survey data. Isn't that enough?"

‣ "I run a really strong team meeting each month and I'll ask the questions there. That's the best I can do."

‣ "Shouldn't HR be doing this?"

‣ "I have too many direct reports to have more meetings."

‣ "Let's tack these questions on the end of the performance review since we already have the employee in the room."

‣ "Shouldn't employees be in charge of motivating themselves?"

‣ And they're probably also thinking: "My boss never talks about my turnover rates or engagement scores so why should I care?"

You've chosen to read this book so I know you'll invest yourself wholeheartedly. Besides, you would never treat your customers with excuses like the ones above, and certainly your employees are as important as your customers if not more so.

## Why Not Ask?

From the treetops, stay interviews put you in command. They are the primary tool to use to learn why your employees stay or might leave, what you can do to improve their happiness and productivity, the destinations they have in mind for their careers, and the degree to which you can count on them for the long term. As managers we get only so many positions, so many "chairs" to fill with people, including ourselves, to produce all the assignments that constitute our jobs. Great managers place total value on all chairs and the people who occupy them to ensure that they perform at their very best and that their best is good enough. Stay interviews provide the insight to *know* rather than have to assume if each employee fits correctly, is motivated to give 100 percent, and has intentions to stick around.

My work with stay interviews has convinced me that they are *the missing link* between managers and employees. After all, if you want to know how to get employees to stay and work harder, you have to go ask them, because they are the only ones who know.

## Notes

1. United States Bureau of Labor Statistics Job Openings and Labor Report citing voluntary quits from 2009 through 2013.

2. Steve Crabtree, "Worldwide, 13% of Employees Are Engaged at Work," *Gallup World*, October 8, 2013, http://www.gallup.com/poll/165269/worldwide-employees-engaged-work.aspx.

3. "Bersin & Associates First-ever Employee Engagement Solution Provider Buyer's Guide Identifies Latest Trends in a Fast-Growing $1.53 Billion Market," Bersin by Deloitte, August 14, 2012, http://www.bersin.com/News/Content.aspx?id=15735.

4. Jim Clifton, *The Coming Jobs War* (New York: Gallup Press, 2011), 11.

5. "Comparative Cumulative Stock Market Returns" figure in "What Are the Benefits?" http://www.greatplacetowork.com/our-approach/what-are-the-benefits-great-workplaces.

# Preparing to Conduct Stay Interviews

s I wrote in the previous chapter, the best way to ensure that you conduct a successful stay interview is to prepare beforehand. You can't just wing it and see what happens. That might even be counterproductive because it suggests to your employees that you have better things to do, you don't care about the outcomes, and you have little regard for them. What a way to turn a potential win into a huge loss.

This chapter will urge you to execute every pre-meeting step so that you come out of the meeting with a greater relationship with and commitment from your employee.

## Preparation Step #1: Plan

Start by making a list of all the employees on your team, then placing two columns to the right. Label the first column "Important to Them" and the second column "My Beliefs." Under "Important to Them," list every wishlist item you've heard each individual employee say or that you have reason to anticipate. Consider schedules, workload, pay, their further development, and whatever else comes to mind. Then in the "My Beliefs" column, list topics you'd like to introduce for them if they don't introduce them on their own. These might include a job skill you've seen that they should expand or an activity like mentoring that would bring them joy and help your team as well. The items you place under "My Beliefs" must represent ideas you attach to that employee specifically based on something you've seen in him that you want to explore.

Make sure that your "Important to Them" lists do not include items that are instead important to *you*. Avoid falling into the trap of thinking that if something is important to you, then it must be important to everybody, whether it's pay, promotions, or something else. Conducting effective stay interviews requires putting your needs on the sideline and focusing entirely on those of your employees.

Also get ready for two possible detours during your meetings. The first is obvious: that your employees will introduce ideas that surprise you no matter how well you think you know them. Be flexible in your thinking (no automatic no's), don't be afraid to ask questions to learn more about the topic, and above all remember that the topic may not be important to you but it's important to them.

The second detour is completely within your control. You must avoid converting your stay interview meeting into a performance review. And your best defense is to ensure that all performance issues have been thoroughly discusse d before your stay interview meeting, very openly and entirely up front. There will be times when you need to remind an employee about a recent performance discussion, such as when an employee states a career goal that is currently out of reach, but stating a performance deficiency for the first time in a stay interview guarantees derailment. Stay interviews must be positive engagement-and-retention-building activities. Imagine the fallout from a conversation like this:

**William:** I'd really like to learn more about healthcare coding and be considered for a position in that department.

**You:** Come on, William. You can't do detail work like that. You have errors and typos every month in your production reports.

**William:** Really? I didn't know that. Why didn't you tell me?

Your stay interview meeting has crossed the boundary into a performance meeting and is now effectively over. This discussion would have gone differently if that performance shortcoming had been addressed in advance:

**William:** I'd really like to learn more about healthcare coding and be considered for a position in that department.

**You:** Do you really think you would enjoy that work, William? And be good at it based on discussions we've had in the past about your detail work? Your skills seem more directed at working with others outside of the backroom instead of hunching over detailed reports. Can you think of other skills you want to build?

**William:** Yeah, maybe I should think about that. I've always seen myself as a people person. I just thought I could make more money by coding. What are the best next steps you see for me and my career?

Now your stay interview is on a strong track that will lead to improved engagement and retention.

## Preparation Step #2: Enter with a Clean Slate

Who sets the agenda for each stay interview meeting? Your employees. You are a facilitator, a skilled host who directs each individual discussion, but this is their time to express what is important to them.

As a result, anticipating the topics each employee will bring up can open you up to a major mistake by redirecting the discussion to a topic you choose. Or worse, you might begin the discussion by naming a topic that you believe will be atop the employee's list but may not be. Adding to the risk, you even have a column labeled "My Beliefs," which subconsciously can guide you to easily redirect the conversation to your chosen subjects.

Here's a worst-case way to begin the meeting:

**You:** We're here today to talk about how I can help you become more engaged in your work and stay here longer, Susan. And since every time we pass in the hall you mention how busy you are, I know that's where we should start. Let me share a few ideas for you.

I'll present a better, scripted way to start your meeting in Chapter 4.

## Preparation Step #3: Devise Questions to Ask

Let's differentiate first between questions and probes. Your *questions* should be precisely worded and open-ended, designed to trigger the employee to open her mind to you on the given subject. Your *probes*, then, are your tools for exploration, to gain all of the specific knowledge an employee has to give that enables you to propose the best solutions. Questions are fixed; you should never vary from them.

Probes, though, have no boundaries as long as they stay peripherally on the topic. Probing requires greater skill because your ultimate stay plan's quality will hinge on the depth to which you understand how your employee thinks and what she wants.

I'll present four specific skills that are required for stay interviews in Chapter 3 and probing will be one of them. For now, though, let me recommend the five questions my company's client managers use when conducting stay interviews with their teams. They call these the SI 5:

1. When you come to work each day, what things do you look forward to?

2. What are you learning here?

3. Why do you stay here?

4. When was the last time you thought about leaving our team? What prompted it?

5. What can I do to make your experience at work better for you?

When linked to the right probes, these five questions yield all of the information you'll need, and they should be used during every stay interview you conduct. Here's the reasoning behind each one.

▸ *When you travel to work each day, what things do you look forward to?* This question brings the employee's mind into the here-and-now. Research indicates that the primary drivers of engagement and retention are trusting one's manager, liking one's colleagues and respecting their work, and enjoying the job's duties with some degree of challenge. This question starts the meeting positively and directs employees to think about these day-to-day aspects of their jobs.

Note that the three primary engagement and retention drivers mentioned above—trusting the manager, respecting colleagues, and liking one's duties—are all strongly influenced by the manager.

Inevitably some employees will answer facetiously with, "What do I look forward to? Going back home at the end of the day." I coach managers to respond, "Yeah, I've had a few of those days, too. But seriously, what things do you really look forward to when you travel to work?"

‣ *What are you learning here?* Employee development is considered to be of utmost importance for engaging employees and influencing them to stay. But some employees like what they do, want no complications, and do their jobs well. This question usually leads to a long pause followed by words that both answer it and also give clues to whether the employee wants to learn more.

‣ *Why do you stay here?* In my previous book, *Rethinking Retention in Good Times and Bad*, I made the case that "Employees stay for things they get uniquely from you." Finding each employee's true answer to this question leads to the pot of engagement-and-retention gold. Many employees have never considered this. Skilled managers ask this question and then bring the right probes to unlock the answer.

‣ *When was the last time you thought about leaving our team? What prompted it?* Let's clarify first that every employee thinks about leaving at least once in a while, on a very bad day or just out of curiosity. Asking employees about leaving does not introduce a subject they haven't thought about before. Their specific answer here tells you their leave triggers, topics that have such deep meaning they could leave you because of them. The right probes then tell you if these circumstances still exist.

▸ *What can I do to make your experience at work better for you?* This question might yield a topic for you to investigate such as "When will we get new equipment?" or something much deeper and impactful like a request that you change your management style. The type of answer you get depends in part on how well you probe and also how effectively you've built trust with this employee, both before the stay interview and during it until now.

There have been times when my company has helped client managers add a question or two to specifically address a negative trend on recent engagement or exit survey results. But combined with the right, skillful probes, these questions yield all of the data required to maximize engagement and retention with each employee.

## Preparation Step #4: Have Resources at Your Fingertips

Think for a moment about every employee program your company offers, funded with the full intention that they will increase engagement and retention. Then recall from Chapter 1 where you read that these programs are typically implemented "above and around each employee's direct supervisor"; yet research tells us you are the primary lever for how hard your employees work and how long they stay. Stay interviews provide the opportunity not only to leverage these programs but also to give you ownership of them, such that they now are offered *by you* rather than *around you*.

So what programs does your company offer? Now is the time to bone up on the entire list so you have all the programs fresh in your mind when discussing ideas and developing stay plans. Full information for all of these programs is likely available at your fingertips via your keyboard. Here's a starter list of common programs many companies offer or can make happen by request:

- Job posting

- Career days or fairs

- Tuition reimbursement

- Internal training programs

- Mentoring programs

- Internal input groups

- Presentation opportunities at new employee orientation

- Planning committees for holiday parties and other events

- Employee referral programs and rewards

- Flexible scheduling

- Work from home

- Health programs, sometimes to lower each employee's insurance copays

- Fund-raising walks, Habitat home-building, and other volunteer civic programs

- Professional certifications

- Conferences to build specific skills

- Rotary, Chamber of Commerce, and other professional civic participations

- City and other government board positions

- Company-sponsored recreation teams from softball to yoga

- Participation in company's donation decisions

- Various incentive programs to increase compensation

- Transportation help via ride-sharing, van pooling, or discounted passes

- Company policy for matching personal donations to charities

Now go back to your "My Beliefs" lists and consider which of these programs might eventually find their place on one or more of your employees' stay plans if they meet a specific interest or need for that employee.

## Preparation Step #5:
## Overcome Fears and Defensiveness

You have a fairly accurate idea of topics your employees will present. And even though they will toss you a fresh idea or two, your anticipated responses are likely to be at least 50 percent correct. The great news is you don't have to solve or even respond to topics on the spot. Instead:

### Probe Deeply, Solve Completely

The more surprised we are by something we hear, the more questions we respond with as probes to learn more about it. This applies, too, to feedback we hear about our own management styles. None of us really wants to hear negative things about ourselves, ever, yet stay interviews give us the opportunity to listen, consider, and, if applicable, change our behaviors. Besides, we absolutely cannot build trust if we can't respond to feedback about ourselves with an open mind for change.

Let's role-play a positive and a negative way to respond to this feedback. Here's the wrong way first:

**Sylvia:** You want to know what you can do to make my experience at work better? Well, for one thing, you can stop micromanaging me by looking over my shoulder at my work and checking on me like a third-grade teacher. That's what you can do.

**You:** I only look over your shoulder because sometimes you make mistakes. Besides, I liked my third-grade teacher.

A better response would be:

**You:** I'm sorry you feel that way, Sylvia. Tell me what I do that makes you feel like I check too closely on your work.

As the conversation continues, you might say comments like this:

So I hear you saying that I provide too many instructions, that you don't get to think on your own. Does that sound like a fair description to you?

One example of my looking over your shoulder is when you were preparing the monthly sales report for the board. Can you tell me another example?

It sounds like you would enjoy your work more if you felt more independence, and that when I double-check your work you feel I don't trust you. Does that sound right to you?

The important distinction here is you are seeking first to understand, and you are completely removing your ego from the conversation. It would be easy to fall into the trap of immediately defending yourself, including by making a comment about a mistake Sylvia made some time ago. And it would be emotionally un-intelligent to do so because once she learns you can't take feedback, she will not only clam up but also warn others not to show all their cards. Or, said another way, your employees won't trust you.

Imagine instead that Sylvia gave you some feedback you didn't want to hear and after the meeting she went to the break room and said this to other members of your team:

I had a great stay interview with Monica. These stay interviews are for real. She wanted to know how she could make my work better and when I told her some things she does that irritate me, she listened and asked me to tell her more about it. Once I found she didn't chop my head off, I kept telling her more about it and she took me very seriously.

The important thing about this dialogue is *it does not include solutions*. The exchange above is about one question followed by multiple probes and very good listening. Rather than propose solutions on the spot, imagine having a small STOP sign in your pocket that you can pull out anytime and say:

Thank you, Sylvia, for all you've told me about the way I work. Let me consider what you've said and I want to hear from others, too. I promise to come back to you within two weeks and maybe propose some changes in my style and get your feedback. I very much appreciate your having the courage to tell me these things and I promise to take them to heart.

So your commitment to Sylvia is to consider what she said, get more information from others, and come back to her with possible changes. And not once in the role-play did you say some something defensive; hopefully your facial expressions and body language reflected your true openness, too.

Besides, committing to a quick fix for complicated problems comes off as insincere. From the employee's perspective, responding to any type of complex request with a one-sentence action plan seems like a way to escape the topic and head toward the door. Complex problems require carefully considered, detailed solutions that actually work.

## Preparation Step #6: Invite, Sequence, and Schedule

The best way to invite employees to participate in stay interviews is to first introduce the topic in a team meeting, whether in person or by phone. Here's a script for doing so:

> I have a new idea that I think will make working here better for all of us. During the next few weeks I'm going to schedule a stay interview meeting, one-on-one, with each of you. The purpose is for you to tell me every single thing I can do to make your job better, and I will then make every possible change that I think makes sense and that is within my control. And if something seems right that is not within my control, I'll ask those above me to make it happen. Sounds easy, right?

> So I'll bring a few questions but I want you to think in advance about what is really most important to you. And then let's talk about it. I'll be in touch with each of you to schedule the meeting.

Then after the meeting, contact each employee and schedule a thirty-minute stay interview. Thirty minutes is ideal because it removes time for "filler" discussions and sends a signal that this is a business meeting and the business topic is to help you enjoy your job more. If you like, leave a few extra minutes on your calendar in case the meeting runs over. And remember, of course, that you can always schedule a second meeting if necessary to explore one or more topics in greater detail.

When employees learn the meeting is scheduled for thirty minutes, the implied message is that they come prepared, that they at least identify for themselves one or two things they want to discuss.

This is similar to the practice therapists use to schedule meetings for a defined period of time so patients know the clock is ticking for them to get everything on the table.

Another reason I recommend the thirty-minute limit is because your schedule was stretched before you took on stay interviews as another assignment. Feel free to schedule more time if your interests and schedule permit.

For scheduling sequence, start with someone who makes you comfortable and will likely present ideas you've discussed before. In other words, start with an easy one. Then move to (1) those employees whom you value the most, (2) those who perform well whom you might lose, and (3) the rest.

Thinking longer term, client managers at my client companies conduct stay interviews at least once per year, ideally opposite from the time they conduct performance reviews. They also conduct stay interviews two times with new hires within the "tipping point" period when new hires typically quit. Turnover by length-of-service is reviewed with a targeted eye for first-year patterns to identify each job's tipping point, which reveals that if new hires stay that long they typically stay much longer. By conducting two stay interviews during this period, managers tend to greatly reduce new-hire turnover and subsequently reduce all turnover.

## Preparation Step #7: Choose a Location and Seating

Where is your employee most likely to share new information? I say "new" because great interviewers cause their interviewees to disclose information that is even new to the speaker. Your meeting location should be one where the employee feels comfortable disclosing private information; thus, an office or conference room is in order rather than an open space. But where might that employee lose his sense of subordination and really open up? A quiet corner in the cafeteria? The coffee shop across the street? A midday walk around the building?

When I ask managers if they have ever had a meeting with a past supervisor that was just about them and not their performance, very few say yes. So assume this is a one-of-a-kind meeting for each of your employees. What location tells them this meeting is different? If you meet in an office, seating should be in front of the desk rather than with you behind it. Asking for openness requires that you remove that large piece of furniture that often separates you from others.

## Preparation Step #8: Gather Your Equipment

Your only required equipment is an electronic device or paper on which you include:

- Your "Important to Them" and "My Beliefs" notes for each employee.

- The SI 5 questions.

- And the opening scripts, probes for each question, and closing scripts, which are presented in the chapters that follow. Taking notes during the meeting is essential so that you (1) capture all key spoken items, (2) can reference them later when developing your resulting stay plan, and (3) send a clear message to your employee that his opinion really does matter.

## Preparation Step #9:
## Visualize Success. You Are Ready!

You now have (1) your "Important to Them" and "My Beliefs" lists for each employee, (2) your personal commitment to enter each meeting with a clean slate, (3) five highly researched questions you will ask, (4) total re-familiarization with each employee program and a few ideas of how you might apply them to specific employees, (5) guidelines for overcoming fear of surprises and also your own defensiveness, and (6) a detailed plan for inviting, sequencing, and scheduling your team.

Now imagine a few moments from each meeting and visualize success. Many of us have read about "visualizing success" in articles and books and wondered if doing so really contributes to making us perform better in an important future event. It does.

# Four
# Essential
# Skills

ow that you've visualized success, let's make it happen. There are four core skills required to conduct stay interviews effectively: listening, taking notes, probing, and taking responsibility for company decisions. Study this section carefully and return to it after your first three stay interviews to score yourself on your skill-application performance.

## Listening

Listening means more than just using your ears. Focus your entire attention on the speaker. Maintain eye contact, nod your head, and don't interrupt. Hear what your employee actually says. And along the way connect the dots from one thing you hear to another to identify his real opinions about his work experiences.

I learned two tricks in graduate school to show I'm listening, and I use them to this day because they're simple and effective. The first is to say this sentence after an employee—or anyone—says something that is important to him or her:

**"Let me tell you what I heard you say to see if I got it right,"**

followed by repeating the message I heard. This statement also provides a check on your conversation to make sure you and the employee are on the same page. Use it surgically, though; overuse will make you sound insincere.

The second trick is to restate a person's emotion in a way that shows I understand how he feels. For example, if an employee explains how upset he is because his work doesn't seem to matter, an appropriate response would be, "You seem really frustrated that you put in all those hours but in the end the project was cancelled." The employee's response is then something like, "Yeah, you're right I'm frustrated. Who wouldn't be?" The employee, even if upset, will develop a solid trust-building connection with you as a result.

## Taking Notes

Taking notes is essential for the reasons mentioned in Chapter 2, which were (1) to capture all key spoken items, (2) so you can reference them later when developing your resulting stay plan, and (3) to send a clear message to your employee that his opinion really does matter.

Besides, over time you will forget important details, which for stay interviews means you might miss a clue. And one employee's comments might sound like another's so without notes you'll tend to develop stay plans that don't quite fit.

Old-fashioned pen and paper seems to work better than tablets. The movement of eye contact to paper and back feels more genuine to employees than to a computer or tablet where your video game could be on pause.

## Probing

*Probing* requires you to connect many dots, to listen carefully to widely related comments, and then to identify the additional one or two pieces of information that complete the picture in your employee's mind and also your own. That is, great probing leads to fresh discovery.

Probes are usually open-ended and begin with "Can you give me an example?" or "Tell me more about . . . ." While they encourage employees to disclose important information to you, they direct employees to announce new information to themselves, too. Therapists are trained to help patients discover and then state new information during sessions so therapists can repeat it back *so patients know they said it*. Patients, then, or in our case employees, are far more likely to agree with the statement and take actions based on it than they would if you instead told them it was your opinion rather than their opinion.

Another reason to probe is to build trust. I mentioned in Chapter 1 that the absolutely most important trait for leaders on all levels to improve engagement and retention with their teams is trust. Imagine if you conducted a stay interview by asking only the SI 5 and no follow-up probes at all:

> **You:** When you travel to work each day, what things do you look forward to?
>
> **Michael:** I like seeing my friends at work and I also enjoy lunch.
>
> **You:** What are you learning here?
>
> **Michael:** At first I learned a few sales techniques for selling products over the phone, but I haven't learned much since.

**You:** Why do you stay here?

**Michael:** Mostly to hang with my friends. I want a job that's closer to home, but I haven't gotten around to applying for one.

**You:** When was the last time you thought about leaving our team? What prompted it?

**Michael:** About a week ago. It's the closer-to-home thing, the same thing I just told you.

**You:** What can I do to make your experience at work better for you?

**Michael:** I guess move our building closer to my home.

Michael obviously sounds quite disengaged. And you can be sure he has more to say that would unlock clues to increase his production. But the absence of any probes from his manager sends the clear signal that the manager is going through the motions to check the stay interview box. So why should Michael contribute any additional thinking? He'd rather get back to his work buddies and count down the minutes to lunch.

Here's an example of a manager who probes effectively. In this case the manager is conducting a stay interview with Maria, a bank loan officer. This example begins with the manager asking question #4:

**Manager:** When was the last time you thought about leaving our team, Maria? What prompted it?

**Maria:** I'm just so busy. I can't possibly get all of my work done and it stresses me out. I want to do a great job but I carry this stress with me all the time, even at home.

**Manager:** I'm sorry, Maria, that's not good. What are the specific work assignments that bring on this stress for you?

**Maria:** I really like calling on customers and learning their banking needs. And then my favorite part of my job is to sit at my desk with my computer to study their business so I can determine the best way to help them. I feel so good, then, when I have the perfect package of loans and other solutions to help them reach their business goals. But then I cringe when I have to present my package to the loan committee, because they ask so many questions and sometimes they turn me down.

**Manager:** What's the worst part of getting turned down by the loan committee, Maria?

**Maria:** I feel like I've let my customer down and I haven't done my job. And it's no fun being grilled in front of my peers.

**Manager:** Yeah, I can see where all of those things would feel bad. Which part would you say is the worst part, Maria? Is it letting your customer down or being "grilled," as you say, by your peers?

**Maria:** It's the grilling part. I go into the meeting thinking I'm fully prepared but I'm not. And then I leave embarrassed.

**Manager:** It sounds to me that the worst part of all is feeling embarrassed. Would you say that's true?

**Maria:** Sure it is. How would you like it if the people you work with every day told you you were wrong?

Bingo! Whereas Maria began by saying she had considered leaving because she was over-worked, good probing led her to discover the cause of her problem, which in the end was not about being over-worked at all. From this point Maria and her manager will design a stay plan that includes her learning to be more prepared for her loan committee meetings and also growing thicker skin when hearing feedback from her peers.

When Maria began by saying, "I'm just so busy," a less-skilled manager would have presumed Maria had too many assignments and then would probe to identify which ones to remove. Or that same manager might ask Maria if she put enough hours into the job. But by asking, "What are the specific work assignments that bring on this stress for you?" this manager opened Maria's thinking to ultimately identify that work stress was not from too much work but instead from very specific work that made Maria uncomfortable. Now together they can build a plan to address Maria's greatest job concern. And as important, Maria will fully buy into the plan because she just listened to herself identify her problem.

The greatest lesson from this manager's probes with Maria is this: When employees express over-arching, broadly stated concerns like "too much work" or "I'm so stressed," there are usually one or two activities or relationships that drive these emotions. In this case the ultimate stressor was Maria being "grilled by her peers." Great probers don't accept broad-based concerns but instead find that pearl in the oyster that leads to real solutions.

One way to think about probing is to borrow language from two classic business books:

Roger Fisher and William Ury formalized the process of negotiating in *Getting to Yes*.[1] Their principled negotiation points include "Focus on interests and not positions" and "Invent options for mutual gain." Applying these principles to stay interviews leads me to think great probers dig deeply by asking questions, and they move the conversation beyond initial summary statements like "I'm just so busy." Then great probers suspend judgment to not color what they hear. That way they unite with their employees to discover truths that lead to productive solutions for both.

In *The 7 Habits of Highly Effective People*, Stephen Covey taught us that great historic leaders would "Seek first to understand, and then to be understood."[2] I took this message to mean *probe to see the other person's perspective so you can then if appropriate adjust your own*. And, as important, provide solutions that meet the employee's needs as well as yours.

These examples make clear that probing effectively leads to developing the right, on-target stay plans, and that deep, skillful probing builds trust by itself.

Three standard probes for each of the SI 5 follow. These are optional, of course, depending on the responses you hear from your employees. Feel free to invent your own, too.

1. When you travel to work each day, what things do you look forward to?

    a. What do you like most about working here?

    b. What parts are the most challenging?

    c. What do you least like about working here?

2. What are you learning here?

    a. Is there anything else you'd like to be learning here but are not?

    b. How do you learn best? By doing? By observing? By attending training?

    c. Do you feel like you can advance your career here if you want to?

3. Why do you stay here?

    a. Is that the only reason?

    b. How much does the type of work you do impact your decision to stay?

    c. How much do you stay because you like working with our customers? Our team?

4. When was the last time you thought about leaving our team? What prompted it?

    a. Does this still concern you?

    b. On a scale from one to ten with ten being "I'm staying for the foreseeable future" and one being, "I'm leaving ASAP," how would you rate your intention to leave?

    c. What's the single most meaningful action I could take to address this issue?

5. What can I do to make your experience at work better for you?

    a. What should I do more of? Less of? What do I do that frustrates you?

    b. Is there anything I do that strikes you as particularly unfair or unreasonable?

    c. Do you feel like I truly hear your concerns when you have them?

## Taking Responsibility for Company Decisions

You can be certain there will be times during stay interviews when you'll want to throw your company under the bus. A few employees, maybe more, will complain about their pay, their health insurance copays, or the impact of company strategy on their jobs or their customers. Moments like these represent a stay interview gut check because ducking and pointing fingers comes so easily.

The fact is that the employees you want to keep and further engage tend to follow your lead. Consciously or not, they seek signals from you on whether the company is on the right track and whether the company makes the right decisions for the good of all. These employees are usually reasonable and will accept decisions that cause short-term pain for long-term gain. Mostly they want to know what you think, especially if you've build trust with them. And here's another contributing factor: They would rather feel good than feel bad.

So how can you bridge the gap between supporting company policies and at the same time maintaining trust with your team? Surely the answer is not to lie, to stretch the truth, or even to dodge the questions.

The short answer is to become very comfortable with statements such as these:

> **Our executives usually make good decisions, so I support them.**
>
> **The executives who make these decisions always know things we don't.**

Two factors play into you saying these statements. The first is that you must believe them. This does not mean that you must agree with every decision that comes down the pike, but rather that in general you believe your executives are managing your company in the right way. If you do not believe this, address this privately with your manager until you either sincerely convert your thinking or consider if your company is right for you. No organization can reach peak engagement and retention if its managers doubt the company's direction.

The second factor concerns conflicting values at the top and in the middle. If executives were asked about their highest values, I suspect they would say maintaining the company's current value in the short term and growing the company in the long term. But if middle managers and their teams were queried, their highest values would likely be providing outstanding services to customers and ensuring the best possible pay, benefits, and programs for employees. These sometimes conflict and it's one of those subjects that isn't talked about. Maybe that should change.

Ideally, all executive decisions would be communicated clearly and openly to all employees with a complete accounting for all considerations. This doesn't happen, though, and it leaves you in the middle to form your own opinions, as anyone would. You, then, become the conduit for these decisions, and your behaviors help to form your employees' opinions. For many, you are the architect of how your employees see your company and your executives. Stay interviews present just another example of the opportunities you have to influence your team's perceptions.

One last thought: Studies have shown that employees reject top management's thinking when they believe they should have been consulted first. How many watercooler discussions have begun with, "Why didn't they ask me about how this impacts our customers?" Rationally, it is tempting to say "Companies are not democracies so get back to work." But a better solution is to recognize employees' need to give input and to have their opinions heard. Invite their thinking and defuse a situation by saying, "We didn't get to make this decision, but we do get to decide how to make it work in our department. Let's all meet here tomorrow at 4:00 and everyone bring at least three good ideas." Now you've restored their pride and sense of purpose.

## Notes

**1.** Roger Fisher and William Ury, *Getting to Yes*, 2nd ed. (New York: Penguin Books, 1991).

**2.** Stephen Covey, *The 7 Habits of Highly Effective People* (New York: Simon & Schuster, 1989).

# Managing the Exchange

et's start with the opening lines. The following opening remarks are scripted to achieve three objectives:

1. To tell your employee the purpose of the meeting

2. To limit the employee's expectations by narrowing her suggestions to things you can control rather than actively inviting conversations about pay, benefits, and other areas where you have less influence, even though you will leave the door open to discuss them if these are important to the employee

3. To ensure that your encouraging words do not become a legally binding contract, such as by your guaranteeing an employee a job forever when what you meant was that you hope she stays for a long time

Here, then, are the recommended opening remarks, in sequence:

My primary interest for our time today is to learn what I personally can do to make this a great place for you to work.

So based on our meeting, I hope we will work together here for a long time and you are fully engaged in your work.

As you know, our company, like all companies, has policies for which I can make recommendations but don't have the authority to change, such as pay, benefits, and the like. I still want you to tell me what is important to you regardless of whether I can change it, but I'm going to be listening especially for things I can control, things that I can do something about.

Client managers at my company use these scripts, but feel free to use similar phrases to let employees know your purpose as well as the limitations of your authority. Then they are more likely to provide ideas back to you that you can control.

## Sample Scripts and the SI Mantra

In Chapter 2 I introduced this mantra to make stay interviews effective:

### Probe Deeply, Solve Completely

By "Probe Deeply" I mean dig for the information that will help you build the spot-on stay plan to improve your employee's productivity through greater engagement and also retain her longer. Your ultimate goal is to create a discovery experience through your probing that causes this employee to hear disclosures she finds within herself in the meeting. "Solve Completely" means uncover every stone to deliver the best solutions possible and, when necessary, consult with your manager and others as appropriate. "Completely" also means bring the best solutions, even though they might require a second meeting to fully explore possibilities, be imperfect, or even disappoint your employee.

Let's explore five scenarios for conducting stay interviews with (1) a satisfied employee, (2) a mystery employee, (3) a low-performing employee, (4) an overly ambitious employee, and (5) a high-performing employee. These scripts will emphasize the power of the SI mantra; then I'll present the lessons learned from each. I'll begin each example with a different question from the SI 5, working from first to last.

## Scenario #1: Satisfied and Steady

Sheila has trudged to the mall for over four years now, selling watches and other jewelry and occasionally crossing the aisle to the fragrance section. As her manager, you'd score her performance as "good enough" on most days, with an occasional burst of outstanding customer service. Throughout your career you've seen others like her build their sales skills to increase their pay, volunteer for extra shifts, and pitch in to check inventory. Two of Sheila's peers have been promoted to shift supervisor.

Preparing for your stay interview, your "Important to Them" page is blank because Sheila has never indicated a desire to do more. Experience tells you you'd far rather keep Sheila than lose her because the quality of the applicant pool for this type of job is, well, shallow. So your pre-meeting question for yourself is, "Am I doing all I can to engage and keep her?" Let's look in on your stay interview meeting beginning with SI question #1.

**You:** Sheila, when you travel to work each day, what things do you look forward to?

**Sheila:** I love walking into the mall and into our store when it's quiet. When there's not yet a buzz and everything is perfect. The floors are shiny, the shelves are fully stocked, and even the clothes are neatly folded over in women's fashions.

**You:** It sounds like you're a grown-up "mall rat." Is that fair to say?

**Sheila:** You know, I've looked forward to coming to this mall since I was five years old. I tell my friends I can smell the mall. Some of my best times in high school were right here when we would meet after school or especially on Friday nights. It was like one big group date. It didn't matter what we did, we were just here and it made us feel okay.

**You:** So let's visualize you driving to the mall and parking your car here, Sheila. What are the things that you *don't* look forward to? What are the parts of your job you don't like?

**Sheila:** I always remember that one customer from the day before who went away disappointed. Maybe it was because we didn't have the perfect gift. Sometimes guys feel that pressure to find just the right thing, and I want to help them find it. But that just makes me think about how to help the next customer who comes in.

Based on this dialogue and the description before it, Sheila finds high energy each day she when she comes to work at the mall, and she wants to keep doing exactly what she does. As the meeting continues, you would ask her the remaining four SI questions about learning, staying, potentially leaving, and how you can help, but Sheila is content. She has established hours, a steady job, a steady paycheck, and work activities that make her happy. The best you can do in this meeting is repeat back all she's told you and ask her to approach you if she has future ideas, questions, or concerns. And know you've done the best you could.

Months from now, Sheila might send signals that work has become redundant, and you would re-ask the SI 5, but for now all appears to be very okay.

## Scenario #2: The Mystery Employee

David was hired fresh out of a top-level university to join your computer programming team. He had many choices because his skills were in great demand. During your pre-hire interview, you sensed he could hit the ground running and make a major dent in backed-up work that was keeping a highly anticipated new product from launching on time. You were accountable for a major share of this launch and David's skills gave you every indication he could be your salvation. And he was.

Now, nine months later, you are implementing stay interviews with your team. Since your initial pre-hire meeting, David has said little about himself and shows emotion only when using the tech-talk jargon that accompanies his job. He has performed well enough that you must retain him, and you also know headhunters seem to have your programming team on speed dial. Another team member drops hints about her own headhunter calls, and her credentials pale next to David's. You must use your stay interview to retain him without knowing his ideal career path or even if he wants a major pay hike based on his initial achievements. Let's begin the discussion with SI question #2.

**You:** So David, what are you learning here?

**David:** Well, this is my first real job so I've had to learn how "work" works, you know? How to get along with others, how to connect with a boss, how to budget my time, how to meet deadlines. Much of it has been like college but it's all more formal, more structured.

**You:** So how about it being "more structured," as you say? How do you like it so far?

**David:** It's all fine. Everyone's been nice to me. But it's all peripheral to my real work, which is programming. That's what I like to do.

**You:** So tell me why programming is so special to you, David.

**David:** It's the challenge. It's like building one big jigsaw puzzle with the built-in complexity of technology. I start from a broad perspective by asking what is the total assignment? What is it that I'm making here? And then I have to dig into the technical details.

**You:** How do you keep yourself fresh? Do you ever ask others on the team for help?

**David:** Not usually. They're all nice, but I keep all of my textbooks on the shelf behind me. And I have software packages on my own laptop that I check all the time for unusual programming tips.

**You:** So theoretically, David, if I could remove all of the people around you, all of the desks and chairs, and even I stayed out of your way so all you had to do was program, would that be okay?

**David:** Okay? That would be ideal! Since my first computer class in high school programming was all I wanted to do.

**You:** What else would you like to learn about programming, David? Are there specific courses you'd want to take, either online or through a school?

**David:** Can I show you my list?

Attuned listeners will readily grasp David's professional turn-on. He likes focused, challenging work and creates his own feelings of achievement. Fresh knowledge feeds this drive while people and other surroundings are distractions. Others might crave this environment but need more direction that only humans can provide, but your experience with David is "so far, so good." Your probes have led you to the top solution for retaining him at this point in his career: more knowledge. But you also know you need to keep checking in should his interests change.

## Scenario #3: Low Performers Need Hope

Your assisted living center performs in the middle of the pack compared to others on the corporate list, and you've determined that three of your department heads' jobs are in jeopardy. One of these is Robert, who oversees admissions. Robert is a plodder despite his significant knowledge of social work and the industry. Your conversations about this have been direct and clear so now he faces the dreaded "get better or get out" dilemma.

Yet you believe that Robert merits a stay interview, too. One reason why is that you haven't given up on him, but the more commanding reason is that he will give up on himself if he hears that you are having these meetings with others but left him out. So you've begun your meeting by reminding him of the performance feedback but encouraging him, too, based on your confidence that he can get his performance back on track. Let's begin with SI question #3.

> **You:** So Robert, given everything we've talked about today and in the past, why do you stay here?

> **Robert:** That is such a good question. I'm really burned out in admissions. It's just the same tedious conversations with family members every day about how we'll treat their parents and the like.

> **You:** When those conversations become tedious rather than sensitive, Robert, then you really are burned out.

> **Robert:** Yeah, I get that. I stay, though, because I like helping sick people, and I like the security that a large and stable company brings. I'm just in the wrong job. I need a challenge, to use my mind more than I can right now.

> **You:** A year ago, Robert, I had an idea that you could move into marketing and become an outside person rather than an inside one. I could see you joining Rotary and spreading the consistent word throughout our community that we do a top-notch job. I even imagined you coming to me with fresh ideas to improve our bottom line. But then your performance fell off a cliff.

**Robert:** So how can I get back into your good graces? What must I do to have that opportunity in marketing or some-where else that's different?

**You:** There's good news and other news, Robert. Our company has several facilities in town and there are always a few opportunities for you. But you must first perform your job better. You must come in here on time with high energy. And most important, those meetings you called "tedious" must become inspiring events for family members so they leave here with total confidence that their family member is in the right place. Can you do that?

**Robert:** I can do that. Now that I see the carrot I am much more motivated to do my job better.

**You:** That's good, Robert. I'll be watching.

Some might wonder whether to conduct a stay interview with someone who's on his way out the door. Sometimes low performers are just wrong hires and you need to let them go. But at least as often, their situation drags down their performance—from poor training, a bad job fit, or a jerk boss. In this situation, Robert might pull himself out of his nose-dive. But he might not because he continues to fail and his manager won't risk moving him to another job until he shows a spark. Robert's future, then, is up to him.

When managers properly prepare for stay interviews and then probe deeply, solutions can make themselves available that save talent and further engage it. In this example, you as the manager have responded to Robert's reasons for staying as effectively and honestly as you can.

## Scenario #4: Ambition Overload

Your call center team has more turnover than you and your manager would like but you take mild comfort when seeing the same data from competitors. You wonder if the industry trend of hiring young workers contributes to the challenge.

Today you meet with Tyler, who is six months into his job and ready to manage the world. Tyler's first career move out of high school was to register for community college but two courses later he lost interest. His performance so far is medium and your challenge is to retain him, engage him more, and tone down his expectations. He sees his future more clearly than his shortcomings. Let's begin with SI question #4.

**You:** When was the last time you thought about leaving our team, Tyler? And please tell me what prompted it.

**Tyler:** I'm always on the lookout for more opportunity, more money. Gotta make that car payment. One of my buds told me about a job hanging doors that pays $15 an hour.

**You:** That's interesting. What about your work here prepares you to hang doors?

**Tyler:** Nothing. Well, I guess working with people, which you have to do to hang doors.

**You:** So would you leave call centers to do just about any other work in order to make more money?

**Tyler:** Well, I wouldn't want to put shingles on roofs in August, ya know. Don't get me wrong, I really like working here. But I don't know my next step. When do I become a supervisor? How can I make more money? How soon can I tell my friends I do more than talk on the phone all day? This company just doesn't see my talent.

**You:** It's my job to see your talent, Tyler, not the company's. For starters, you have improvements to make in your calling techniques that we talked about a few weeks ago. I suggest you place your full efforts there to show you can improve and also show your commitment to us. Otherwise it sounds like you are just shopping around for any job that pays more money. Is that fair to say?

**Tyler:** Well, not really. I just hear stuff and wonder about it. But seriously, what does it take to become a supervisor?

**You:** What qualities do you see in James, your team lead, that make him successful?

**Tyler:** James is cool. He's always there when we need him and he tells us things that are helpful without making us feel bad. He always encourages us.

**You:** Why don't you make a list of every good quality you see in James and all of our supervisors and then we'll discuss your list. Let's make a plan to meet again next Tuesday.

Would you expect Tyler to be there a year later? Neither would I. As manager, you addressed head-on his disloyalty, which caused him to peel back and say he only thinks about leaving rather than acts it. So your on-the-spot outcome was to remind him of performance improvements—ones he had heard before—and give a leadership development assignment. How much you rely on him will depend in part on whether he actually does that leadership assignment.

Note, too, that when he blamed his career woes on the company, you stepped in and took responsibility instead. You then reminded him of the previous improvement feedback because he needed that redirection, but you did not specify it to avoid switching your stay interview to a performance meeting.

Sometimes stay interviews are effective because they provide warnings. In this example, Tyler might leap onto the opportunities provided here even though he likely sees them as homework. Or you might learn he's probably a short-timer and, thus, drive harder to hold him accountable for good work while you have him.

## Scenario #5: High Performers Need Rope

You are a plant manager whose six direct reports perform their jobs on different levels and in different ways. But Tanya, who oversees quality control, is your gem. She has been with you for just two years and has clearly distinguished herself as the strongest problem-solver, and when you are elsewhere Tanya is the assumed leader in the eyes of the others. In fact, your hopes for promotion to the largest plant depend in part on Tanya's continued growth as well as your ability to retain her.

Preparing for Tanya's stay interview, you feel yourself on edge. Her style is direct and she's used to getting what she wants. Experience tells you many high performers handle themselves this way and you need to be ready for what she brings. Let's begin this final scenario with SI question #5.

**You:** Tanya, what can I do to make your experience at work better for you?

**Tanya:** Let me check my notes. The first thing I want is for you to hold the other supervisors accountable for quality work because when they screw up it makes my numbers look bad. If I'm in charge of quality but they report to you, then I need you to do your job better.

**You:** Help me understand this better, Tanya. Can you give me an example or two of how I'm not holding the supervisors accountable?

**Tanya:** We both know that Harvey's team performs the worst, and also that he sits in his office down there and hardly knows his people. His quality numbers are in the tank and when corporate sees those reports they probably wonder why I'm not doing a better job with quality since I'm in charge of it. How would you feel?

**You:** So let me tell you what I heard you say to see if I got it right. You want me to take action against Harvey until he cleans up his quality numbers.

**Tanya:** You got it.

**You:** I completely agree, Tanya. I can't tell you any actions I've already taken because that's confidential, but you should continue to bring this to my attention if you don't see change soon. So how else can I make working here better for you?

**Tanya:** I want to reorganize my department based on the strengths I see for each person on my team. For starters, I want to establish a clear second-in-command, and that would be Johnson because he . . . .

Tanya brought many pages of notes, so you can envision how this scenario unfolds. She is loaded with ideas and most of them are good. Some of them, too, will separate her from her peers because her organization chart might be different or she could even propose unique working titles for her employees. Your role is to retain and engage her within broad reason while knowing she will continually challenge you in ways that, for the most part, increase your own productivity and therefore your career progression.

The greatest lesson in this chapter is to *Probe Deeply, Solve Completely.* The fictional scenarios make clear that employees bring much more information to their stay interview meetings than they usually put on the table, in part because they haven't yet articulated the answers to your probes themselves. So you are both hearing many of their responses for the first time. There are other lessons here, too:

- Some employees want nothing more from you and that's okay.

- Others have more ambition than commitment, and you need to push them to get on or off the bus.

- One stay interview meeting might convert a low-performing employee to a good one because you showed you still cared about that employee's success.

- A few heads-down employees give few everyday clues regarding satisfaction until you ask them.

- High performers drive your success, but sometimes you must succumb to their egos.

Sound familiar? This is the people-style environment in which we work, because humans come in all forms and sizes. Our job as managers is to continually refine our own skills to drive team productivity and therefore our own success.

# Developing Stay Plans

he five scenarios presented in Chapter 4 are based on actual stay interviews conducted by managers at my client companies. As the managers probed deeply to solve completely, they drew out the information they needed to use to retain their employees. The actions they and the employee must take based on this information is called the *stay plan*. This chapter will show you how to build stay plans.

First, a few ground rules:

‣ Stay plans work best when built mutually by you and your employee. You might review your stay interview notes and develop an idea or two to address your employee's needs. The next best step is to present your ideas in general and then gain your employee's additional input. Your plan should include precise activities each of you will do and dates you will meet. This way your employee buys in fully from the start.

‣ Building the right stay plan for each employee is the next link in the chain for building trust. Your listening, note-taking, probing, and company-supportive statements have positioned you to form or solidify the bedrock of your relationship. Proposing the right stay plan further embeds this trust.

▸ Stay plans work best when customized for each employee. Stay interviews look for the button unique to each employee that when pushed engages and retains, so a one-size-fits-all solution would be ineffective.

▸ To design these unique stay plans, each must be tilted toward individual employees' strengths and preferences: how they learn, how they like to be recognized, and what conditions enable them to perform at their best.

▸ Not every employee will want or need a stay plan. Mall-rat Sheila is content in her role and your only assignment is to continue to verify this is true by checking in every few months. Sheila might also send signs that she is weary of her job's redundancies, which would be a clue.

▸ Building stay plans for a few employees will require a second meeting or even a third. Helping an employee build specific skills to reach a desired career level could require that you investigate internal and external training options while she considers the ideal career outcome she wants.

▸ Sometimes your answer must be "no." There are reasonable boundaries for all desires. Pay comes to mind first but the same might apply to development, new roles, schedules, and other topics. Most employees understand these boundaries when they are carefully and tactfully explained. And a few will ramp up their production because you at least asked and considered their query.

‣ Some employees are immune to giving their all or committing to your company. Tyler from the call center may have slipped through your hiring processes but he'll hang around until his spirit moves him to leave.

The really good news is that stay plan solutions are not a "fixed pie." When doling out pay increases, each manager must decide who gets what, and some must get less than others. Building creative, effective stay plans, though, provides plenty for all.

## Real Change Happens Bottom-Up

You can't dictate a stay plan. It has to be a response to what the employee wants and that will require you to make your organization responsive as well. This can be a challenge, so here are three model bottom-up solutions of increasing difficulty.

The first is the easiest. An employee is looking for an opportunity that requires you to seek help from others: your manager, HR, a peer manager, or another person in your organization. For example, your employee in a manufacturing production job might be taking online marketing courses and want to learn more about job opportunities there. You may hardly know the marketing director, Beverly, but you'll have to ask if she can accommodate your employee's request. If she's performing stay interviews herself, she'll certainly understand. She may even have someone in her department who wants to explore a career in production.

A more difficult challenge is accommodating an employee where you lack authority. In this example, you manage Ross, who is your star software engineer with three years of service. During the stay interview, Ross told you that he knows a few other software engineers in the department have stock options and he believes his performance is better, even though he comes up short compared to them on age and length of service. You agree with Ross in your heart and also know you need his production to get the latest version of your product to market on time. What to do?

At this point in your stay interview meeting, you should tell Ross you must do some homework and schedule a second meeting. Next, you should consult with your manager to verify if Ross's information regarding stock options is true. Assuming so, you've now appropriately shared your dilemma with your manager, who might go further up the chain. The critical fact here is: *Ross is essential to your achieving your goals.* Your responsibility is to communicate to your manager and if appropriate those above your manager that Ross's knowledge about others' stock options is correct, that he outperforms the others, that you will miss your target without Ross, and that other jobs are available to Ross with companies that likely do provide stock options.

The outcome might be that Ross gets stock options immediately, you disclose a timeline to him to get them, or you have to tell him that he can't have the options. In the latter case, you should point out that he asked for something beyond your authority, and you acted as his advocate, but your request was denied. You must do this assertively and without sugarcoating what happened. Then you must support your company's decision.

The third bottom-up solution involves challenging company policies, for instance, employee schedules. While a few companies have tossed out schedules completely and permit employees to work when they want, others require employees to work on fixed schedules that begin and end at approximately the same times. There's a good chance at least one employee will challenge this if you work in a fixed-schedule company, especially if you live and work in a large urban area where commuting can be a challenge.

In Chapter 2 I suggested you investigate all company resources in advance and "flexible schedules" and "work from home" are on that list. For these topics it is good to know your company's *practices*, too, because there might be some managers or special situations that permit employees to work on different schedules than the rest even though no formal policy says this is acceptable.

So let's imagine that as you conduct stay interviews, three members of your team present the idea of coming into work at different times in order to accommodate child-care obligations or to avoid rush-hour traffic. You see ways to change schedules for these employees and make the same opportunities available to the rest of your team. You should check, however, with your manager to ensure that you are not violating a written or unwritten company rule. If necessary, your manager would ideally then push upstream for reasonable policy changes across the board that would make your company a better place for all employees to work.

These bottom-up solutions are the way policy changes originate in most companies. Continuing with the schedule example, few CEOs or HR directors come to work one day and decide to toss out schedules. Instead, they react to employee requests and listen most carefully to their top performers. And since stay interviews are now your way of asking what your employees want, you can expect requests like these and others that will ultimately change your company's policies . . . in a very good way.

## Myths and Truths About Development

When asked about stay interviews some managers say, "We do development plans," as though they are the same. Development may be more important to some employees than others but it is far from the only thing employees look for from you.

"Development" has different meanings for different employees. For some it means promotion to a new role and more money in their pocket. Others see it as a way to stimulate their minds and fend off daily boredom. And some are simply naturally curious and want to learn new things.

Many of us reflexively associate development with courses. Companies reinforce this by listing "tuition reimbursement" as a benefit without specifying other methods they offer for employees to learn.

The very good work of leadership gurus Michael Lombardo and Robert Eichinger shines a bright light on how employees learn and the relative unimportance of coursework. Based on their research, they say the following:

> Development generally begins with a realization of current or future need and the motivation to do something about it. This might come from feedback, a mistake, watching other people's reactions, failing at or not being up to a task—in other words, from experience. The odds are that development will be about 70 percent from on-the-job experiences, working on tasks and problems, about 20 percent from feedback or working around good and bad examples of the need, and 10 percent from courses and reading.[1]

Some employees must complete courses for required job certifications such as in healthcare. For others, though, much learning is available inside your building. Besides, courses cost money and internal development is free except for the solid investments of time you and others devote as teachers. And many organizations have hundreds of teachers. The example above where we connected a manufacturing employee to the marketing department is an ideal example of a manager taking the lead to provide a legitimate development opportunity for his employee.

## Building Tight, Mutually Responsible Stay Plans

Stay plans must contain the following components:

1. The objective for each initiative

2. Actions you as the manager will take

3. Ideally, actions the employee will take

4. Dates for each, and in some cases multiple dates for multiple activities

5. Everything put in writing with copies given to you and the employee

My experience indicates no stay plan should include more than three objectives.

The reason employees should have assignments is so they have some skin in the game. Salespeople know that customers appreciate products more if they pay for them versus get them for free. Look back on Tyler from Chapter 4: You as his manager asked him to come back with a list of the best qualities he saw in other supervisors. This was partly a test to see if he would really invest himself to earn consideration for promotion to supervisor.

Let us lean again on our mantra: Probe Deeply, Solve Completely. All stay plans must connect the vital dots between what our employees tell us and the solutions we recommend. Here is a list of top employee wish-list subjects, three probes for you to dig deeper, and then a few possible solutions, unless your answer must be "no."

Note that some of the solution lists include actions for both you and the employee. Consider this a "starter list" for your thinking because your probes and solutions will ideally be more specifically targeted to meet the unique needs of your employee.

| SUBJECT | PROBES | SOLUTIONS |
|---|---|---|
| **Communication** | What information do you need? How do you like to receive information? In meetings? One-to-one? By email? What are subjects for which you want to provide input? | Schedule weekly individual meetings. Solicit input for team meeting agendas. Commit to communicating specific information more quickly. Nominate employee for a specific-topic input group. |
| **Company direction** | What specifically concerns you about our company's direction? Is there one decision or event that prompted your concern? What other perceptions are you hearing or reading that might be influencing your own perceptions? | Provide press releases and other relevant information. Ask a senior manager to meet with employee to clarify company direction. Invite senior manager to speak at a team meeting and take questions and encourage this employee in advance to surface any concerns. |
| **Conflicts with peers** | What's the origin? When would you say was the first time you felt uncomfortable? What role might you have played in this conflict? | Coach employee to change behaviors. Bring employee together with others involved in conflicts to resolve issues openly. |

*(continued)*

| SUBJECT | PROBES | SOLUTIONS |
|---|---|---|
| **Conflicts with peers** *(cont.)* | What do you wish you had done differently? What outcome do you want? | Worst case and if employee is a high performer, rearrange work relationships. |
| **Development** | If you could learn about just one additional topic related to your job, what would that one topic be? How do you learn best? By reading? Listening? Observing? Doing? How can I know that our plan is working, that you are learning what we both want you to learn? | Assign a mentor for a specific number of hours each week for a specific period of weeks. Ask employee to identify relevant books and web-sites. Recommend internal and/or external courses. |
| **Job duties** | If your job could be nar-rowed down to just three duties, what would they be? Or just one duty? Tell me more about why doing that creates stress for you? What one additional skill would help you feel better and be more productive? | Ask employee to demon-strate how your com-pany's productivity would improve if she focused on doing just that one duty. Propose a skill-building plan to reduce job stress. Arrange job shadowing with a high-performing peer. |
| **New role/promotion** | Tell me the perfect job for you. Why is that job so appeal-ing to you? What skills do you have that qualify you for that job? | Ask employee to meet with/shadow incumbent in desired job and report back on five most impor-tant skills. |

| SUBJECT | PROBES | SOLUTIONS |
|---|---|---|
| **New role/promotion** *(cont.)* | What skills would you have to build? | Give employee specific feedback on her skill levels and skills needed. Build plan to develop skills via mentoring, course-work, and feedback. |
| **Pay** | How much money do you think you should be making? What actions do you see that you can take to increase your pay? What skills can you build that would make you more valuable to our company? | Check employee's pay against same-performing peers to verify it is right. Design development plan that is targeted toward a different role for more pay if employee has talent to qualify. Ensure employee knows all incentive opportunities that might provide shorter-term rewards. |
| **Poor relationship with a top manager** | Tell me when you first had this feeling? What role might you have played in this relationship breakdown? What outcome is perfect for you? | Provide feedback to employee on how to impress top manager in the future. With employee's permission, meet with top manager to address issue. Recommend employee meet with top manager and prep both in advance. |
| **Recognition** | Tell me a time when you should have been recognized but you were not. | Commit to lending a sharper eye to identify achievements and recognition opportunities. |

*(continued)*

| SUBJECT | PROBES | SOLUTIONS |
|---|---|---|
| Recognition (cont.) | How do you like to be recognized? In public or privately? How does recognition motivate you to perform better? | Ask employee to come forward privately to tell you achievements you might overlook or might not be visible. Consider employee for monthly or annual achievement awards if performance merits consideration. |
| Schedule | What's the perfect schedule for you? How can you complete your required assignments if you work that schedule? How would your working that schedule impact the work of others? | Consider if employee can maintain same work standards if you approve that schedule. Consider schedule's impact on the work of others. Implement a peer scheduling method where employees can easily change shifts with each other. |
| Too much work | What are the three most important assignments in your job? What can you stop doing that won't be missed? Which assignment gives you the most stress? | Address the narrow list of assignments or relationships that cause the most stress. Eliminate unnecessary assignments. Reassign less-important assignments that are lesser fits with employee's skills. |
| Work from home | How would working from home improve your productivity? | Recommend a specific work-from-home schedule and ask for feedback. |

| SUBJECT | PROBES | SOLUTIONS |
|---------|--------|-----------|
| **Work from home** *(cont.)* | What standards can you recommend that we can measure your at-home productivity against? Who must you maintain close relationships with to be productive and how would you do that? | Consider employee's productivity standards and provide feedback. With employee, identify best ways essential relationships can be maintained. Seek upstream approval if necessary. |
| **Work location** | How would working there make your life better? What roles are available in that location that you could fulfill? What additional skills do you need to secure a position there? | Instruct employee on how to identify open positions in that location. Make contacts for employee in that location to learn more information and potentially visit. Consider and communicate your company's relocation policy. |

Let's close this chapter with a full example of a stay plan, using Tanya from Chapter 4 as our example. She was the high-performing quality manager who challenged you as her manager to hold Harvey and other leaders accountable for their quality. The specific concern she expressed was that "corporate" would see your division's quality reports and hold her accountable for the substandard performances of Harvey and others even though they reported to you. Tanya also challenged you regarding whether you held these managers accountable for their quality scores. Additionally, she said she wanted to reorganize her department including making Johnson her designated second-in-command.

As you listened, probed, and reflected on your notes, Tanya expressed two very different issues regarding Harvey. Whereas she insisted that you hold him accountable, her equal or greater need was *to not have Harvey's performance reflect on her own in the eyes of* *"corporate" when they read her quality reports.* This discovery invites a stay plan objective that was not obvious at first. So as your meeting moves from the probing stage to the planning stage, you say this:

> Tell me, Tanya, while I know Harvey's quality numbers are important to you, how important is my protecting you from corporate so they don't believe Harvey's performance reflects your own?

With Tanya responding "very much," you then propose a first stay plan objective:

> Let me suggest that we agree on a way for me to advise corporate that Harvey's quality numbers and those of his peers are my responsibility and not yours . . . and that I strongly support all of the actions you've taken to position Harvey and others to perform their jobs at the absolute highest quality. Would that make you feel better?

Again hearing a positive response, you then say the following in order to include Tanya in the action planning:

> Tanya, who specifically would you like me to contact with that message? And are there any specific words or examples you'd like me to use to ensure that they understand the message, that Harvey's and others' quality scores do not reflect your work?

Based on Tanya's input regarding who should be contacted and how, you then write down the first objective for Tanya's stay plan.

## OBJECTIVE #1

Notify Marcie Bradley, SVP Corporate, that Tanya has done a top-level job of ensuring that all managers have the complete set of information required to perform at the highest quality levels, and also that Tanya is in no way accountable for each manager's quality scores. I will notify Marcie of this via an email within three business days, and I will also tell Marcie this in person in four weeks when I travel to headquarters for the next division-head meeting.

For the next objective, Tanya has made clear that she expects you to take action against managers with low quality. You've made clear that you cannot disclose actions you take, but you also know that Tanya will feel more involved if she "reminds" you of those who score below the standard when she distributes the monthly quality reports. So for the second stay plan objective you ask Tanya the following:

> Tanya, would you feel more effective in your job if each month you delivered the quality report to me and highlighted those managers who score below our standard? Be assured I read the report each month and I also do follow-up on those who miss the standard, but I'm wondering if that extra step might be good for you and for me.

While you are not sure you need this extra service, you also know Tanya becomes even more engaged when she can wield influence and even control. As important, you want Tanya to have her own responsibilities as part of her stay plan. Predictably Tanya agrees, so the second objective of her stay plan reads:

## OBJECTIVE #2

On the fifth business day of each month when Tanya distributes the quality report for the previous month, she will also deliver to me the same report with highlights indicating which managers failed to achieve their quality goals.

The remaining topic from our scenario was Tanya's desire to reorganize her department and name Johnson as the designated second-in-command. You want to accommodate Tanya's plans but at the same time ensure that her desired appointments, titles, and reporting structure align with your own beliefs, because you are counting on Tanya to continue on the path to become your successor. So after proposing a specific plan to achieve this to Tanya and gaining her buy-in, you script one more stay plan objective:

### OBJECTIVE #3

Tanya will propose her department's reorganization with names, roles, titles, reporting relationships, and communication plan within thirty days from today.

This objective not only meets your mutual need but also provides Tanya with an additional role that will further develop her own managerial skills.

Then to finalize the stay plan process, you email Tanya her stay plan so all next steps are clear, and you also put both your due dates and Tanya's due dates for each objective on your calendar. And to ensure completion, you put a heads-up note for each of your own responsibilities on your calendar three days before they are due.

Effective stay plans, thus, must provide details and also the answers to who, what, and when. "When" provides deadlines and ensures that the plan is completed on both sides.

## Note

1. Robert Lombardo and Michael Eichinger, *The Career Architect Development Planner*, 5th ed. (Minneapolis: Lominger, 2010), iv.

# Closing and Forecasting

n *Rethinking Retention in Good Times and Bad* I referenced my best boss ever, a southern gentleman named Bob Bowen.[1] To this day when faced with tough issues in my life I hear a voice in my head that says "What would Bowen do?" Bob influenced me so strongly because his commitments and actions toward building trust never wavered, through every interaction both personally and professionally during our time together. On top of that, he was and remains the most emotionally intelligent person I've ever known.

After we had worked together for about six months, Bob invited me to his office. Sitting behind a closed door, he said this to me:

"Finney, I want us to work together for a long time so I'm going to make you an offer. If you accept it, we'll shake hands and our bond is our word.

"You're going to have some tough days here because I might be difficult, our team will have conflicts, or management will run us in circles. When those days happen, you might decide to look for another job.

"So here is my offer. If you ever decide to start looking, I want you to promise that you will come tell me on that day. And my promise to you is I will make every effort to make our company a place where you want to stay. But if you ever place an envelope on my desk that tells me you're leaving and we haven't talked about it before, you've broken the deal."

Can all of us make the same type of request at the end of our stay interview meetings? Sure. The difference is whether your employees place enough trust in you to fulfill this commitment. Realistically, no one will say no and all will shake your hand and make this agreement. The "trust" part will drive whether they keep it.

In my case, I stayed with that company another fourteen years and ultimately left just a few months after Bob did. I don't think it's a coincidence. Hence, again, the power of trust.

## Essential Closing Messages

Let's recall the primary components of stay plans:

1. The objective for each initiative

2. Actions you as the manager will take

3. Ideally, actions the employee will take

4. Dates for each, and in some cases multiple dates for multiple activities

5. Components put in writing with copies for you and the employee

Details drive required actions, so stay plans must include *clear objectives* you and the employee both understand, defined activities for each, and dates when activities will be completed. These stay plans might also include intermittent commitments to meet again or ways to track progress. Written, documented stay plans can be delivered at the end of the meeting or shortly after. Sending by email is one way that provides documented communication that if appropriate can be shared with your manager or others you've included in delivering your stay plan.

At the end of the in-person meeting, client managers at my company then say the following to their employees:

▸ "Thank you for discussing with me today why you stay at our company."

▸ "We discussed . . . ," followed by summary statements from meeting notes.

▸ "And as a result, our action plan will include . . . ."

▸ "My responsibilities and timelines are . . . ."

▸ "And your responsibilities and timelines are . . . ."

▸ If scheduling a follow-up meeting is appropriate, say "I'd like to take some time and perhaps consult with others on some ideas you've mentioned; can we meet again at this same time next week?" (or a similar time).

▸ "I hope we work together here for a long time. If for any reason, whether about me, the organization, or your home life, you would consider leaving our company, can I have your commitment that you will tell me first so I can try to solve your problem?"

This final statement must be posed as a question with direct eye contact so the employee will answer. You are asking for a commitment to be on the inside, to be trusted, to be the first or among the first to hear if the employee forms doubts about continuing to work with your company for any reason. One way to view this request is as you asking permission to continue the type of stay interview discussion you've started into the future. And while you will continue to implement your stay plan, follow up to ensure its success, and conduct future stay interviews, this request requires employee initiation rather than your own.

## You Must Fulfill Your Commitments

After the meeting your responsibility is to *fulfill your own stay plan commitments*. All trust-building efforts have no value if you overlook an assignment or miss a deadline without clear and advance communication with your employee.

Breaking stay plan commitments brings to mind the common employee lament about employee surveys:

> We take the time to fill out these surveys, and it's the same thing every year: Do the survey, get a thank-you email, hear some results in a meeting, and then nothing changes.

This is a trust-breaking statement, the type that brings tag-along emotions that linger and drive down performance. The impact of missing a stay plan assignment is much worse, though. When a company does nothing after a performance survey the employees can at least feel disappointed as a community. When you fail a specific employee, that's a personal betrayal.

## Forecasting Each Employee's Retention and Engagement Risk

Salespeople forecast future sales for two reasons: one, to anticipate and implement any necessary strategy changes and two, to drive each salesperson to live up to his or her forecasts.

So imagine the raw power, the additional commitment you will bring to coaching each individual employee if you commit to yourself how long each employee will stay, and also how that employee will complete the next employee survey if your company conducts one.

Client managers at my company forecast how long each individual employee will stay in three time increments: more than one year, six to twelve months, and zero to six months. For simplicity, one year plus is coded as green, six to twelve months as yellow, and zero to six months as red so vivid forecasts can be represented in dashboard reports. Practice has taught client managers at my client companies that looking beyond one year for most jobs is less reliable and that one year is the best maximum increment, because we recommend stay interviews be completed at least annually and the forecast can be reconsidered then.

Executives should pay special attention to forecasts versus job performance for all employees across their companies. Coding your best performer as red is cause for alarm, whereas coding a low-performing employee as red calls for strong performance coaching. As that top-performing employee's supervisor, your next steps would include revisiting your stay plan to ensure that it provides your best chance at retention and then sharing your stay interview results, stay plan, and forecast with your manager.

Forecasting retention brings with it the added push to improve stay interview skills. Once the employee leaves the discussion, task yourself with answering how long she will stay. Going through your notes, you may find something she said that gives a clue but you now question why you didn't probe more deeply. For example, if she quickly mentioned possibly returning to school, why didn't you ask her to tell more about those plans? Was she thinking full-time or part-time? Online or on campus? Locally or far away?

Conducting stay interviews effectively requires developing strong skills and strong habits, honed through on-the-job practice. Forecasting how long your employees will stay after your first round of stay interviews will shine light on other probes you should have asked and details you might have missed, and therefore sharpen your probing skills for your next stay interview.

If an employee does quit, you can compare his "quit" timeline against your forecast. In fact, I believe that managers who visit with supervisors after each voluntary exit to conduct a manager/supervisor exit interview can have a stronger impact than traditional exit interviews done by HR or third parties. Managers bring with them the power of accountability as they visit with supervisors who report to them so this type of exit meeting answers both "Why did the employee quit?" and "What could you have done to keep the employee?" Imagine yourself in such a meeting where good questions such as these are asked:

- Did you see this exit coming?

- How did you forecast this employee?

- What actions did you put in this employee's stay plan? Were they the right ones?

- What lessons can you learn from this exit?

‣ Who else on your team might be vulnerable for the same reasons?

Let's practice retention forecasting by using our five fictional employees in Chapter 4 as our examples. We should acknowledge, though, that in most cases we will know much more information from daily experiences with team members than we have learned in these short fictional case studies. And all information should be included when making forecasts, whether we learn it during stay interviews or from other discussions or sources, or whether we see employees leaving due to performance issues by our choice or theirs.

### EMPLOYEE #1: Satisfied and Steady Sheila: Forecast Green

Sheila gave every indication in her stay interview that she greatly enjoyed her job, to the extent that she had zero requests to improve it. There are no visible reasons to forecast Sheila to leave within one year.

### EMPLOYEE #2: David the Mystery Employee: Forecast Green

Whereas you knew very little about David's level of commitment or his job turn-ons prior to your stay interview, you successfully unlocked the mystery by probing to learn his singular desire to write code and program. You then committed additional training and on-the-job experiences for him to fulfill those needs, and he left your stay interview meeting with an apparently strong commitment to stay.

### EMPLOYEE #3: Low-Performing Robert: Forecast Red

Robert walked into his stay interview knowing his performance was lacking and his job security was at risk. During the meeting he spoke of regaining his stride, but his performance remains off track. It appears likely that Robert will quit or be fired within six months.

### EMPLOYEE #4: Ambition-Overloaded Tyler: Forecast Yellow

Tyler mentioned no specific attractions to his job and made clear he wants to make more money. He is currently performing acceptably but a fair prediction is that he will eventually flame out or find the ambition to look elsewhere.

### EMPLOYEE #5: High-Performing Tanya: Forecast Green

You have more information for forecasting Tanya's retention than the others because you know her stay plan from Chapter 5. Prior to developing that plan you might have forecasted Tanya as yellow because she was clearly frustrated with you as her manager. The stay plan, though, addressed what you learned to be Tanya's top three concerns: her own vulnerability with corporate, her need for you to address low-quality performers, and her desire to reorganize her department. She is coded green because she completely bought into the stay plan and accepted her roles to complete it.

To be sure, retention forecasting is not scientific. The objective is for you to set reasonable goals for how long your employees will stay based on the information you learned during your stay interviews, the amount of impact you anticipate your stay plan will bring, and other information you learn day-to-day. Yet forecasting brings with it added incentive to probe during stay interviews, to develop better stay plans, to have high antennae for daily clues, and to focus your attention to make your forecast accurate. And most important to take actions that move reds and yellows to greens for those you want to keep.

## Forecasting Engagement

The Gallup Corporation is the world's leading provider of survey data, and one specialty is surveying employees' levels of engagement. Like most engagement survey companies, Gallup stratifies data into three levels of employee engagement, which they call "engaged," "not engaged," and "actively disengaged."[2]

In Chapter 1 I mentioned how U.S. employees' engagement levels have hardly budged. From 2000 to 2013, the percentage of engaged employees has ranged from 26 percent to 30 percent.[3] That is, fewer than one-third of U.S. employees are engaged in their work. More important for us is Gallup's name and definition for the middle group, which is the largest group. These "not engaged" employees are "sleepwalking through their workday."[4] This group is far larger than the "actively disengaged," who are the employees who subtract from productivity and are easier to spot. This middle group is the one you should coach and then, if they don't step it way up, fire.

I believe your primary job regarding each employee's engagement is to move the "not engaged" employees to "engaged." Some survey companies mask this data by changing the terms, calling the top group "highly engaged" and the middle group "engaged." But I trust Gallup's data and therefore its definitions. And if your team's productivity aligns with the data presented here, most of your employees are doing enough work to get by but are not contributing to productivity or revenue in a significant way. They don't provide spark.

So if your company conducts employee surveys, I recommend you forecast whether each employee will score in the top group, or "top box." We borrow this term from those who conduct consumer surveys and watch carefully how many consumers rate products or services at the highest possible level—for example, how many consumers rate products a 9 or 10 on a 10-point scale. Your forecast question is therefore, "On the next employee survey, will this employee score in the top box?"

Of course, most employee surveys are anonymous so you'll never know how each employee scores. So why would you forecast data for which you'll never know if you achieved that forecast? Here are three good reasons:

1. You will likely learn your *team* engagement score even though you won't learn each individual's engagement level, and that team score indicates how many of your employees scored their own engagement levels in the top box.

2. Your alternatives are to either forecast an overall engagement score or make no forecast at all. Forecasting an overall score is akin to picking a number out of the air with no specific vision of how to attain it. And making no forecast reduces your own commitment.

3. The main purpose of forecasting is to sharpen your focus on each individual employee. When asked if Shirley who codes healthcare services all day will score in the top box, you become far more focused on identifying the specific things you must do to improve Shirley's engagement in her everyday job.

Let's apply this idea by forecasting whether each of the same five fictional employees will score in the top box in your next engagement survey. You are certainly limited regarding the amount of information you know for each but these are the forecasts I would make. Again, the question is: "Will this employee score in the top box in the next engagement survey?"

### EMPLOYEE #1: Satisfied and Steady Sheila: Forecast No

Being "satisfied and steady," Sheila shows no signs of becoming a breakout star performer. More important, you were unable to gain a clue from her regarding how you could raise her levels of energy, enthusiasm, or commitment. You learned that her performance was "good enough on most days with an occasional burst of outstanding customer service." Until you unlock Sheila's added potential, if indeed she has it, she is unlikely to become a top-box engagement performer.

### EMPLOYEE #2: David the Mystery Employee: Forecast Yes

David's stay interview provided far more helpful information than Sheila's. By probing deeply you learned David's ideal professional work style and then built a stay plan to provide it for him. Based on what you know, you should have every confidence that David will score as engaged in the next survey.

### EMPLOYEE #3: Low-Performing Robert: Forecast No

Robert talks of regaining his performance edge and you've provided coaching and incentives to help him find it. But he has shown no evidence of applying himself to his work in greater ways.

### EMPLOYEE #4: Ambition-Overloaded Tyler: Forecast No

Your greatest challenge to further engage Tyler is to identify a job in your company that he really wants to do. Your stay interview provided no additional clues and you have reason to believe that Tyler will exit by his choice or yours prior to the next survey.

**EMPLOYEE #5:** High-Performing Tanya: Forecast Yes

Tanya brings energy and ambition and she truly likes her work. And she now knows her greatest needs have been addressed by the smart stay plan you mutually developed.

Forecasting engagement for each employee is harder than forecasting turnover, because the outcome data is foggy versus crystal clear. But the value of doing so brings me back to forecasting's purpose, which is to drive your own focus, your own listening, probing, and ultimate stay-planning, in order to increase each team member's productivity as well as engagement scores and continued retention.

## Moving Forward

Let's envision two scenarios for moving forward, one on your own and the other with your manager.

You've now conducted stay interviews with each member of your team, developed individualized stay plans to which you are devoting your full commitment, and forecasted each employee's future retention and engagement. Each employee's retention and engagement outcome then tells you how effectively you conducted your stay interview except for circumstances that are clearly beyond your control.

Outliers will occur, such as employees quitting abruptly because of real, immediate changes in their life circumstances. And some employees won't stay or engage because they represent hiring mistakes. But in most cases your employees' retention and engagement is driven by their work environment: Do they trust you as their boss? Do they like their colleagues and respect their work? Do they like most of what they do each day? The challenges their job brings? The knowledge they gain?

For this group you are driving their retention and engagement bus. You may adjust your stay plans along the way because your stay interview discussions will set the tone for additional employee conversations later and you will learn new things. Your measures of success are whether you achieve your individualized retention and engagement goals and whether your department's productivity spikes as a result.

## Presenting Your Work Upstream

"Managing up" is an essential skill for career progression. To this point all of your efforts have been about managing down with your teams to increase their productivity, to get more out of each chair. But smartly managing up is required for your ultimate payoff—to get credit for your team's increases in productivity rather than have those increases be assigned to luck or market forces. And this particular type of credit says you can retain, engage, and lead a team: the essential executive skills.

Some might say, "If I do my job well, those above me will take notice." While that might usually be true, I would still announce that I am now conducting stay interviews with my team in a professional way rather than leave getting credit to chance.

So let's foresee your upcoming meeting with your manager. This meeting should be conducted verbally rather than in writing and hopefully in person if logistics permit. Scheduling a special meeting is ideal but it is fine to add this to another agenda as long as adequate time and your manager's complete attention are available. Here's a sample script to get you started:

> I want to tell you about an endeavor I've begun with my team members to improve their retention, engagement, and ultimately their productivity. I've conducted an individual stay

interview with each of them. I now fully understand what drives them and what inhibits their performances, and I've developed a stay plan for each one that we've mutually agreed to. Our company offers many advantages for learning and solving problems and I think I've leveraged these advantages pretty well, and along the way invented some new employee solutions, too.

In addition, I've also forecasted how long each employee will stay with us and how that employee will score in our next engagement survey. I plan to continue conducting stay interviews at least once each year with my team and will also conduct them two times with new hires.

Let me walk you through the highlights of my stay interview meetings with each employee and I'll share their stay plans and forecasts, too. I look forward to your feedback along the way.

From here you can present data for each of your direct reports with emphasis on actions each of you are taking to solidify that employee's place in your company and possibly prepare him or her to contribute more. Your manager might make additional suggestions or even volunteer to engage with some members of your team as an additional part of your stay plans.

Most important, your manager will leave this meeting with new information about you that she will then add to the accumulation of data about your performance and your future opportunities . . . and likely share your stay interview initiative with those above. And the best compliment will be when your manager asks you to share your stay interview methods with peer managers so they can apply your magic and all see you as the leader of this fresh-thinking solution.

## Notes

1. Richard P. Finnegan, *Rethinking Retention in Good Times and Bad* (Boston: Nicholas Brealey, 2009).

2. Gretchen Gavett, "Ten Charts That Show We've All Got a Case of the Mondays," *Harvard Business Review*, June 14, 2013, http://blogs.hbr.org/2013/06/ten-charts-that-show-weve-all-got-a-case-of-the-mondays/.

3. Ibid.

4. Ibid.

# Avoiding the Thirteen Stay Interview Traps

o far I've made stay interviews look easy by presenting preparation tips, required skills, and scripts to help manage each type of exchange. Don't be fooled, though, by their apparent simplicity. Stay interviews can be conducted ineffectively and hurt your team's productivity rather than help it. Let's look at thirteen traps to avoid at all costs.

## During Preparation

### TRAP #1: Fearing Response

Managers who view stay interviews with suspicion usually fall immediately into the first trap, fearing response. They believe that every employee will complain about pay or something else the manager cannot change and therefore the employee will leave the meeting less engaged and more likely to leave. Most managers who hold this opinion also believe that the employee will like them less as a result. And some managers, unfortunately, avoid any interaction that could include conflicts.

Years of experience have taught me that the far more likely outcome is that your employees will be so pleased you care enough to ask these questions that their responses will be about subjects that are more day-to-day, that impact them more frequently than pay. The recommended introductory scripts and the SI 5 also provide a piloting system that directs employees *away* from hard-to-change topics and *toward* more immediate ones.

But let's explore a worst-case example where an employee says, "I deserve more money. What can you get for me?" Chapter 5 provided three probes and three possible solutions that will solve this issue for most employees. To refresh, the probes were:

- How much money do you think you should be making?

- What actions do you see that you can take to increase your pay?

- What skills can you build that would make you more valuable to our company?

And the actions were:

- Check employee's pay against same-performing peers to verify it is appropriate.

- Design a development plan that is targeted toward a different role for more pay if employee has talent to qualify.

- Ensure that employee knows all incentive opportunities that might provide shorter-term rewards.

This approach is *reasonable* in that any employee who has a clear reading of his contributions and his potential will work with you to chart this course toward more pay. More pay might not happen soon, though, as additional development would likely be part of the plan.

But let's carry this "worst case" further. If I managed this employee and valued his contributions yet learned his compensation expectations were outside of his performance or beyond my company's philosophy, this is information I would want to know. Avoiding a feared pay discussion is akin to skipping a doctor visit when pain from an unknown source continues to throb. Sometimes we need to know what we don't want to know.

This type of pay confrontation rarely happens during stay interviews, for all the reasons stated previously. But when it does, manage it, embrace it, and learn that your employee might be a flight risk because he has unrealistic expectations about his pay.

### TRAP #2: Bringing up Hidden Performance Issues

Recall from the example in Chapter 2 that introducing a performance issue during a stay interview for the first time immediately redirects your meeting to a performance management discussion, thereby ending your stay interview. Performance issues need to be surfaced if an employee's ambition is outside the scope of her performance, but they must be *resurfaced* rather than stated for the very first time, and only if absolutely necessary. Hearing the phrase, "You never told me that" is a sure sign that your stay interview just reached its end.

### TRAP #3: Tipping the Agenda

Preparing an "Important to Them" list for each employee and then setting it aside during the meeting creates a conundrum. Wouldn't it be easier, you say, to just cut to the chase and get to the issues you know the employee really cares about? The answer is "no," of course, because writing out the "Important to Them" list prepares you for possible outcomes, but you can never permit yourself to set the meeting's agenda. The SI 5 and probes provide structure, but the employee must drive the content of every one of your stay interview meetings.

### TRAP #4: Being Sketchy on Company Resources

I provided a list of potential resources in Chapter 2 and it is your responsibility to know them, detail by detail. How many days must an employee wait to job post after moving into a new position? How many months must an employee wait to earn her full employee referral bonus after the referred candidate is hired? Which courses are considered "job-related" and what percent of tuition does the company pay? And for executives, how long must a young gun stay on board before her stock options vest?

Passing the quiz on these questions indicates that you know your company's *policies* but knowing your company's *practices* is just as important. How far has my manager stretched on allowing employees in other departments to work from home? Must I get higher-up approval for my employees to work nontypical schedules if they still get their work done and their lives are easier as a result?

## During the Meeting

### TRAP #5: Forcing the Meeting

Let's start with an easy one. This comes into play if a top manager or peer begins conducting stay interviews before you and then "suggests" you implement them, too. Imagine the motivational difference between these two invitations:

I'd like to schedule a meeting with you to focus entirely on you. What do you like about working here versus anything you might dislike? How do you feel about working with me versus something you want me to change? I really want to learn what I can do to make this company and this job the absolutely best it can be for you.

And:

William over in marketing has begun doing this thing called stay interviews, so Virginia thinks this is the hot new management idea and told us all we have to do them. Let's schedule a meeting so I can get these done.

As a rule, if you're a having a meeting to have the meeting, don't have the meeting.

### TRAP #6: "Conquering" Silence

Don't interrupt the stay interview to alleviate your own discomfort. I recall a counseling professor once saying that if you don't hit a wall or two of silence with probes, you are asking lousy probes. Remember the hourglass icon on the original computer software you may have used? Picture your employee in hourglass mode, sending a nonverbal message to you that reads "I'm digging very deeply here." This is very productive silence.

Your best move is to stay silent too and maintain eye contact with a smile. It is okay after a few seconds to say, "Take your time. I'm very interested in your answer." These are moments when employees are learning more about themselves, and their ultimate response might represent fresh thinking in the form of new information for both of you.

## TRAP #7: Losing Focus

Realistically, some of your employees are more interesting than others, and you actually like some of them more than others, too. It is easy, then, to think back to a deadline you need to meet or to last night's TV show rather than nod appreciatively toward an employee who specializes in saying the same thing over and over. The best solution is to write the same thing over and over in your notes because it keeps you focused.

## TRAP #8: Becoming Defensive

This is an easy one to fall into. You likely have a good idea which employee will tell you something you don't want to hear, either because they have courage or lack emotional intelligence, so brace yourself for the hit during your stay interviews with them whether you feel the hits are deserved or not. Listen and show respect. The short-term pain is worth the long-term gain.

To avoid defensiveness in a meeting, probe, probe, probe, all with an inquisitive look and voice: *Tell me what I did that made you feel that way. Had I ever done that before? What exactly did I say on that day? How many times do you recall that I mentioned this to you?*

Probing does not admit guilt but shows your interest in learning your employee's opinion on what is likely the most important subject to that person. If you believe that you are being accused unjustly, tell her you want to fully consider all she has said. Then wait a few days and revisit her to tell your side. Fight the urge, though, to have your stay interview meeting spill over into a conflict. The long-term gain is represented by watercooler talk where that employee says to others, "Yeah, I told him exactly how I feel about it and you know what? He listened. He actually took notes, asked me more questions, and he listened."

### TRAP #9: Throwing Your Company Under the Bus

"Your company" here might mean your manager, the CEO, or anyone you can potentially blame to shield yourself from your employee's rant about a policy or action he thinks was unfair. I mentioned in Chapter 3 those two sentences we should place under our pillows so they never leave us in times of stress: "Our executives usually make good decisions" and "They always know things we don't."

These sentences won't mollify your employee, nor will they replace a longer discussion about the outcomes of a particular decision. Patient listening is part of the solution here, but ultimately your employee will want to know where you stand and it is very okay for you to say you were not privy to all the particulars but in general you support those at the top.

Contrast this with the manager who immediately wipes away any association with the executives by saying, "Yeah, I'm with you on that one. What were they thinking?" He thinks he just gained points but he lost them. You don't want to be that guy.

### TRAP #10: Solving Quickly

This is the opposite of the mantra Probe Deeply, Solve Completely. When presented with a problem you may be tempted to try to solve it fast and get out of the room, especially when it comes to a high performer who you fear will bring up pay or a long talker who already consumes too much of your time. Quick solutions are like buying cheap furniture. Soon you will be sitting on the floor.

Remember that you need 100 percent of the available information in order to address your employees' needs. Bring to each meeting the courage to ask, listen, and probe in order to put all issues on the table. You might solve them all, too, in their time.

## After the Meeting

### TRAP #11: Building a Lousy Stay Plan

All of the skills you've demonstrated to ask, probe, listen, and take notes have zero value if your plan doesn't address the things that energize your employee to stay and work harder. In addition, if you don't involve your employee in developing the plan and follow-up actions you'll diminish the result. By studying each of your stay plans two weeks later you will likely find you did a more complete job on some than others and brought a spark of creativity to only a few. Feel free to return to each employee and introduce a new idea. What is a better way to say you care?

### TRAP #12: Dropping the Ball

Never will your follow-through be more carefully scrutinized than when you make a stay plan commitment, especially by those who do not easily trust you. So put commitments on your calendar multiple times and accept no excuses from yourself.

## The Thirteenth Trap

Let's take a look at our twelve traps and see what they have in common:

1. Fearing Response

2. Bringing Up Hidden Performance Issues

3. Tipping the Agenda

4. Being Sketchy on Company Resources

5. Forcing the Meeting

6. "Conquering" Silence

7. Losing Focus

8. Becoming Defensive

9. Throwing Your Company Under The Bus

10. Solving Quickly

11. Building a Lousy Stay Plan

12. Dropping the Ball

You could say they all represent bad management habits and you would be right. For me, though, what all these traps have in common is that they can destroy employees' trust in you. Why you fell into a trap doesn't matter from their point of view. Trust is too fragile. A break is a break.

So let's call Trap #13 Breaking Trust. To conduct stay interviews effectively and to grow as a manager, you must have solutions to trust-breaking issues in your pockets at all times. Be prepared to listen carefully, apologize when necessary, and take strong supportive positions even when they might not be popular. All of these equate to the type of manager you want to work with and the type your employees want to work for, too.

# Experienced Managers Tell Their Tales

very stay interview is different, just as is every stay interviewer, so I'm turning this chapter over to our experienced client managers to give you a broader perspective on the process. I've asked them to give you the inside scoop of precisely what happens when they ask, listen, take notes, and build stay plans, so you'll know what to expect yourself.

The responses reveal two trends that don't surprise me. While respondents represent different industries and different cultures, stay interviews prove to raise engagement and retention levels in all corners. In addition, the employees talk mostly about their jobs: the parts they like and don't like and the processes that drive their everyday behaviors. So regardless of where you work, stay interviews should work for you.

## Leila Lassetter, Call Center Executive with Dialog Direct

Leila manages the Denison, Texas, site for Dialog Direct, which provides outsourced customer service for major clients. Leila's center has 400 employees and she has participated in more than 100 stay interviews.

*How frequently do you and your managers conduct stay interviews?*

Most of my managers and I conduct stay interviews every three to four months. This time frame is the right length to realize progress and reinforce our commitment to the employee's well-being.

*What's the best success story you've had that you wouldn't have had without conducting that particular stay interview?*

Once a stellar employee began distancing herself from others and through the interview I discovered she was recently involved in a domestic violence situation and was living out of her car. She had not bathed in some time and was apologetic because she did not want anyone to be bothered by her smell. I was honored that we had built a relationship of trust where she shared such a personal story and was also glad I could help her back into a path of recovery.

Another time we had an employee who was being loud and physically upset with everything and everyone. When we met I put down my pen and asked him "Are you okay?" He began to sob and tell me how hopeless he felt, saying nobody cared whether he lived or died. I said "I do." That was the moment our relationship changed. He trusted me.

*Have you ever improved overall team productivity by conducting stay interviews?*

We had an entire department that was struggling with team attendance. Individual coaching and counseling was not effective. It was through stay interviews that we discovered some of our own workforce practices that were responsible for much of the absenteeism. Not only were gaps identified and closed but employees became mini consultants in helping to find the proper balance, adjusting schedules to meet business needs.

*What's the best probe you've used to get an employee to be more open?*

One of the best probes that my team and I use is to ask employees to describe their ideal job/work environment. Another one is to compare and contrast from that employee's previous stay interview meeting. For example: "The last time we talked you said . . . . How do you feel about that today?"

*What was your greatest fear before you conducted your first stay interview?*

I was worried about my reaction to honest, raw, personal feedback, that I had the strength to just listen and not react or attempt to explain the "why." And that my body language would stay in line despite any feedback I heard. Over time I found if I acknowledged mistakes and truly wanted the feedback, the employee was less likely to beat me up but instead deliver the feedback in a positive manner.

I also feared my inability to actually resolve their issue. I quickly found that they just need to know that their concern has been heard. Most often they give you ample time to research solutions or even help you with a solution.

*How often do employees mention pay as a major issue?*

While pay comes up often in initial discussions, very few employees mention pay as the major issue.

*How often do employees keep their end of the deal by completing their own assignments from your stay interviews with them?*

More than 80 percent of employees and managers keep their end of the deal on next steps from stay interviews. There is always a small percent where we are not well aligned and fail.

*Have you ever regretted conducting a stay interview with an employee?*

Stay interviews are an investment in time but I have never regretted a stay interview. At the end of the day there are few surprises but a lot of intelligence. Recognition, flexibility, consistency, appreciation, tools, and knowledge seem to fall in the top consistently, but each has its unique expectations and outcomes.

## Tara Townsend, Director of Rehabilitation and Wellness Department, Burcham Hills Retirement Community

Tara manages a team of professional healthcare workers in East Lansing, Michigan. She and her managers have conducted over 120 stay interviews. Burcham Hills employs about 400 people.

*Would you say stay interviews have helped you reduce employee turnover?*

With stay interviews we are retaining 95 percent of our full-time staff versus 73 percent in 2012. We also conduct stay interviews two times with new hires and have not lost any employees in their first 90 days, whereas we were losing a full 12 percent during that time earlier.

*What's the best success story you've had that you wouldn't have had without conducting that particular stay interview?*

An employee indicated she felt stagnant, not satisfied with the responsibilities in her job. As a result we agreed she would develop larger, community-wide projects every two to three months that involved research and planning—her strengths—and she would also supervise an intern so she could share her skills and knowledge. These changes increased her productivity and her overall enjoyment with her work.

*What's an example of how you saved a valuable employee from leaving your company by conducting a stay interview?*

During a stay interview a manager said she disliked her management duties by scoring them as a 6 on a 10 scale. Her passion was providing clinical care and we were able to restructure the department and offer her a full-time clinical position with no pay reduction.

*What's an example of how you significantly improved an employee's engagement or productivity by conducting a stay interview?*

An employee identified a concern with communication between the orthopedic surgeons and our therapy team. We created a document for therapists to complete and send to the surgeon for follow-up appointments. The surgeons approved the form prior to implementation to ensure that it met their needs. This new method of communicating greatly improved timely notification of any status changes in the rehabilitation plan of care.

*What's the best skill you've used to get employees to speak openly and honestly with you?*

First is to allow silence. If I wait and give them time, employees usually open up.

And the second is honesty, as I explain I need help to become a better manager so the employees' open feedback helps me to improve. I also don't react negatively when provided constructive feedback from them so that they know they can discuss these issues with me without fear.

*What is the best stay plan you've ever developed? What was the outcome?*

My managers and I developed a tracking tool to ensure that we followed up on our employees' interests, training needs, goals, and concerns that we learned from our stay interviews. We share this information with all employees so they know we have interest in what's important to them. Overall morale and engagement is much higher as a result.

*How often do employees mention pay as a major issue?*
Very often.

*What was your greatest fear before you conducted your first stay interview?*
Two things: Fear employees would say they are actively looking or even tell me they were quitting, and also that they would tell me only what I wanted to hear and would not give me honest answers. Neither of those fears has come true.

## Greg Holmes, Senior Systems Architect with Geocent

Greg is responsible for business management and administrative functions as well as staff planning and employee mentoring. Greg has conducted about fifteen stay interviews. Geocent provides technology services mostly to federal and state governments, is headquartered in New Orleans, and has about 200 employees.

*What's the best success story you've had that you wouldn't have had without conducting that particular stay interview?*
One employee told me during his stay interview that work was taking a real toll on him. He had been working for multiple clients simultaneously, sometimes having to switch context multiple times a day, and he was our only resource on all of these projects. And the isolation of working by himself had him longing for the companionship of a team. I then reassigned him to a team working on a longer-term project. We also needed him to stay on some of the single-resource projects, and he did them more effectively.

*What's an example of how you significantly improved an employee's engagement or productivity by conducting a stay interview?*

One employee confided he was having difficulty dealing with a consultant from a different company who was working on the same project because of her domineering personality. I joined him in a meeting and was able to make sure his voice was heard. He became more confident and contributed more of his ideas going forward.

*What's the best skill you've used to get employees to speak openly and honestly with you?*

I usually have the interview guide printed out and in my hands. The questions usually feel unnatural compared to a casual conversation I would have with a colleague, but instead of pretending otherwise, I acknowledge the awkwardness of it by saying, "These questions may sound a bit awkward, but let's just start with these and see where it takes us." That seems to take the edge off and make it seem less formal.

*What's an example of an employee's response that caught you off guard?*

Our employees are required to earn certain industry certifications. One employee suggested he should be able to spend at least some work hours preparing for the exam instead of all of his studying happening on his own time, after hours. I brought the concern to management and we plan to include some exam prep time in next year's budget.

*How often do employees mention pay as a major issue?*

Pay was not mentioned once in any of the interviews I conducted.

*How accurately can you predict what employees will tell you?*

I could probably predict 80 to 90 percent of what their concerns are. Even if the remaining percentage is small, whatever they decide to hold out until a stay interview is usually going to be very important.

## Leanne Manring, Manager with Madison County Hospital

Leanne is director of the Emergency Department, Oncology Services, and House Coordinators for Madison County Hospital, which is located in London, Ohio, with 280 employees. Leanne has conducted about thirty stay interviews.

*What's an example of how you saved a valuable employee from leaving your company by conducting a stay interview?*

I had a nurse who worked in the Emergency Department who was very skilled and compassionate, and also starting to experience burnout. At the time I had a need in the Oncology Department so I asked if she wanted to continue to work part-time but to try something completely different. She made the transition and has completely overhauled the Oncology Department. She was able to find a niche in nursing that really fits her.

*What's the best probe you've used to get employees to be more open?*

I find that if I let employees know ahead of time that we will be doing stay interviews, explain what the stay interview will entail, and my expectations of them, they are prepared and better able to open up. To probe for more information, I find sharing something about myself helps people open up, particularly if it relates to the situation. And to be honest, I keep a bowl of M&M's on the corner of my desk. Candy always gets people talking.

*What's an example of an employee's response that caught you off guard?*

I had an employee who was in school to complete a bachelor degree. When I asked where she saw herself a year from now, she mentioned a large teaching hospital in a major metropolitan area to do case management, as she did not think there would ever be an opportunity for that job in our smaller hospital. We had a nurse in that same job who was planning to retire so I asked her if she would be interested in job shadowing with that nurse. She said yes, and she later transitioned to that position.

*How often do employees mention pay as a major issue?*

Most will answer that they would like their pay to be better but 90 percent of them say that other factors keep them here. They would not trade the higher pay that larger facilities offer for the hassles that must be endured from working for those facilities. That's why stay interviews have helped us keep turnover very low: because they help us identify issues that are important to our employees, which are also ones we can fix.

## Tushar Ghoshal, Chief Technology Officer, HRsoft

Tushar oversees all technology work for HRsoft, which develops and sells talent management software for organizations and their HR departments. Tushar has conducted more than thirty stay interviews. HRsoft is located in Maitland, Florida, outside of Orlando, and has forty total employees.

Tushar is native to India and began his career there, and he also returns to India frequently. During our interview he also discussed the high value stay interviews would bring to the Indian businesses and overall economy.

*How much have stay interviews impacted your turnover?*

A very high amount. Since committing to stay interviews two years ago we have retained 96 percent of our technology team, which represents a 20 percent retention improvement compared to before we implemented stay interviews.

*What's an example of how you saved a valuable employee from leaving your company by conducting a stay interview?*

An employee with less than six months of service came to see me to resign. The employee cited health issues as the cause, but I believed there were other contributing factors. Mostly I was kicking myself as I had neglected to conduct a stay interview after her first three months. Nevertheless, I met with her and instead of an exit interview I conducted my standard stay interview. Amazingly, we were able to turn things around, avoid the resignation, and develop a stay plan that included reducing her number of projects and permitting her to sometimes work from home. Now that employee is still with our organization and performing very well.

*What's an example of how you significantly improved an employee's engagement or productivity by conducting a stay interview?*

Once I was surprised to hear from a longtime top performer that he felt de-motivated because I didn't push him for deadlines as much as I did in the past. We both laughed that he was going through "workaholic withdrawal symptoms." We immediately built a stay plan where the first task was to find projects he would feel motivated to do and would help move our product roadmap forward. That did the trick. He is very motivated now.

*What was your greatest fear before conducting your first stay interview?*

That employees would steer the conversation toward pay and benefits. Some employees do push a little, but they have much more to reveal about what can keep them motivated and what will make their jobs more satisfying and rewarding.

*What is the easiest mistake to make when conducting stay interviews?*

Being defensive about their responses can be detrimental or even get confrontational. It's important not to pretend about transparency, frankness, and openness but to actually be open to criticism directed toward anybody, including oneself.

*Would stay interviews improve employee engagement and retention in India?*

I can see tremendous potential for stay interviews in India, where the attrition rates are skyrocketing in lockstep with booming opportunities all around for the high-skilled, English-speaking workforce. I started my career in a major IT consultancy firm in India and experienced firsthand the visible and invisible costs of high turnover. If companies combine a conscientious hiring process followed by a diligent stay interview process, they will curb a lot of unnecessary churn while improving employee morale.

## Serena Wright, Director of the Community Wellness Department, Native American Health Center

Serena and the Native American Health Center provide healthcare services primarily to the Native American communities in Oakland and San Francisco, California. Serena has conducted six stay interviews and her company employs 270 people.

*What's the best success story you've had that you wouldn't have had without conducting that particular stay interview?*

A staff member who was very much on the fence about her position was debating whether or not to leave to pursue an independent business. As a result of our stay interview, we agreed on a plan to support her continued role for another year and even transition her into a different part-time position in the agency.

*What's an example of how you significantly improved an employee's engagement or productivity by conducting a stay interview?*

One employee who had been with the agency for a number of years faced significant challenges in the workplace. Shortly after becoming her supervisor I conducted a stay interview with her and this was the best thing I could have done! Taking the time to sit down and talk about what was important to her in the workplace and why she stays here ended up being highly motivating for her. She has now gone from being a mid-level performer to a highly productive, functional, and effective manager.

*How often do employees mention pay as a major issue?*

Almost none have mentioned pay as a major issue.

*How accurately can you predict what employees will tell you?*

I have been surprised at how hard it is to predict what an employee will say. Sometimes the issues can be surmised from observation and prior interactions, but overall I have gained a large amount of insight into the issues that are most important to our employees. Many topics are as unique as the individuals, whereas others are clearly systematic and need to be addressed broadly. My overall experience with stay interviews is that I was just amazed at what people will tell you if you just ask.

*How surprised are you by the things employees tell you are important to them?*

I have been surprised by the range of things that come up, and many of them are simple, straightforward items to address. For example, many employees want to talk about the benefits and challenges of our workplace culture, and for most the solutions come by talking things through.

## Victor Vendetti, Managing Director, MSA Australia, and Business Leader, Oceania Region

Victor is the General Manager for MSA in the parts of our world noted above. Victor has conducted about thirty stay interviews. MSA manufactures and sells safety equipment globally, has 5,300 employees, and is headquartered in Pittsburgh, Pennsylvania.

*What's the best success story you've had that you wouldn't have had without conducting that particular stay interview?*

Prior to my arrival we had 25 percent sales turnover, and with the help of stay interviews we've had near perfect retention since. This is especially gratifying as we've had a few rounds of "redundancies" and other organizational changes but still kept the key people. Stay interviews gave me the opportunity to explain why we made changes and how these people were part of our future, and to do so one-on-one. And they stayed.

*What's the best probe you've used to get employees to be more open?*

After I learn about something important to them I ask, "What would you do if you were me?" This moves their perspective from their role to mine so they then view their request from a higher management level. Sometimes, too, they come back with really good ideas that I not only implement but also know they back the solution because they created it.

*What's the best skill you've used to get employees to speak openly and honestly with you?*

Establishing trust and being rightly humble by saying "I don't have all the answers, and I need your help." Then if at all possible I use that person's ideas to show my words weren't just lip service and the employee's ideas are valued. Even when we can't accommodate something, the employee knows I at least looked into the idea but couldn't do it for whatever reason.

*What was your greatest fear before you conducted your first stay interview?*

That people wouldn't buy in. That I wouldn't be able to meet their expectations. I didn't want to turn this into a career-counseling session, because I know there are more issues out there than careers. Mostly I wanted to learn what makes them decide to come to MSA every day instead of another company.

*What is the easiest mistake to make when conducting stay interviews?*

Not doing the pre-work of setting the meeting expectation. People must enter the meeting with an understanding that we are here to talk about them and not me.

*How often do employees mention pay as a major issue?*

Not mentioned at all during formal stay interview sessions, probably 25 percent of the time during informal discussions.

## Ngozi Adebiyi, Lead Consultant, OutsideInHR

Ngozi Adebiyi is the lead consultant with OutsideInHR, located in Lagos, Nigeria. Ngozi was invited by Fieldco Limited to conduct stay interviews with some of the company's top performers. Fieldco provides integrated property services and has sixty employees.

While the preferred stay interview method is that managers conduct their own stay interviews with their employees, Ngozi nevertheless found very interesting results.

*How important is learning new skills in employees' decisions to stay?*

More important for some than others. What is interesting is some point out job skills and others point out people skills. On the "job" side they speak of learning electrical skills, procurement, and various skills related to a technician. Yet others consider the skills they are learning to be tolerance, patience, extroversion, how to balance perspectives, and how to leverage the tools and skills available versus ones they sometimes wish were available.

*What are the main reasons employees tell you they stay?*

Broadly speaking, it's culture. They stay for the comfort of working with each other, knowing and enjoying familiar faces. Achievement and development contribute, too. They make clear they do not stay for the pay, which they think is low, yet they could take their talents elsewhere but rarely do. Their leaders establish a culture of trust and it is reinforced downward. That's really why they stay.

*So why do they tell you they might leave?*

Most indicate they either do not think about leaving or that they raised an important issue and it was resolved. One employee said, "When I joined I set a goal to leave in five years and now it is six, so I guess I'm staying." Another employee indicated communication was very important to her and she wished top management shared more information and was also open more to her feedback.

*Overall, what were the most common concerns you heard?*

While a few mentioned pay, other concerns were specific to their day-to-day jobs. Some want more clarity in their roles because they feel stretched to achieve all of their assignments. Others indicate they needed better tools but this is now resolved. More training was mentioned by a few. Others want more defined career paths, yet a few want more autonomy. Their overall concerns were about tools, skills, and support methods that lead to their being more productive. That's what made the stay interview experience so enlightening for me. They just want to do their jobs better.

## Karen Smithson, Human Resources Director, Atchley & Associates, LLP

Karen Smithson is the human resources director for Atchley & Associates, LLP, a CPA firm with forty-six employees located in Austin, Texas. Karen is reporting on stay interview results for her managers who have conducted their first stay interviews with each of their employees.

*What was your greatest fear before you conducted your first stay interview?*

We hoped employees would focus on issues their immediate manager could solve versus those outside of their manager's control, those firm-wide issues that are normally addressed at the top. Our hope was the stay interview discussions would concentrate on the individual manager/employee relationships, and for the most part they did.

*What's the best success story you've had that you wouldn't have had without conducting that particular stay interview?*

One of our employees wanted more responsibility but ultimately recognized that she didn't have the required complex problem-solving skills. This led her to have open conversations with her manager, which first resulted in a reassignment and eventually she left us, voluntarily. Her coworkers understood that we tried to advance her but she changed her mind and resigned. We considered the outcome a good one.

*How often do employees mention pay as a major issue?*

Only twice have employees mentioned pay, and both said they would have to be offered a significant increase to leave due to compensation alone.

*How surprised are you by the things employees tell you are important to them?*

Many employees told us that one of the reasons that they stay is because we provide them with opportunities to interact with clients and to be assigned to increasingly challenging and complex work. They told us that they would leave if this changed or stopped.

*What is the easiest mistake to make when conducting stay interviews?*

By far the easiest mistake to make is to fail to probe deeply enough to learn what employees really think. Our managers over time have learned from experience that deep probing requires the courage to ask tough questions and then wait through the silence to learn the most critical information.

# Based on a True Story

et's close with a nearly true story about a manager named Violet. The tale below includes best-case and worst-case experiences I've seen managers work through by conducting stay interviews with their teams. By enhancing their skills over time, these managers grew talents in some employees, promoted others, fired a few, developed succession plans for those who merited them, and devised back-up strategies for those who proved undependable. That is, they learned all there was to learn about each employee and acted on that knowledge to build stronger, more productive teams over time, and they distinguished their careers as a result. But some missteps were made along the way.

Violet is the chief nursing officer for Roaring Falls Medical Center. She reports directly to the CEO and has six direct reports, who oversee nursing departments that are titled Emergency, Surgery, Maternity, Intensive Care, Med-Surg for patients who are recovering from surgery as well as general admittances, and a separate Oncology treatment center. Hospitals compare themselves by number of beds and Roaring Falls is a 292-bed facility.

During her first round of stay interviews, Violet asked the right questions, listened carefully, and built stay plans she would grade as "at least okay." She forecasted that all of her team would stay at least another year and that four of the six would score in the "top box" on the next engagement survey.

The first clue that she was only partially on track came three months later when Buster, her Surgery manager, resigned because he "needed a change" and the competing hospital "offered more money."

Violet reviewed her notes and stay plan for Buster and realized they lacked substance. Items such as "budget for improved equipment" with detailed equipment names, numbers, and dates seemed to please Buster then, yet were completely disconnected from his soon-after resignation for "needing a change" and "money."

Smartly, Violet next reviewed her notes and stay plans for her other five direct reports and found a common trend. Most discussions were about things and not about relationships. Her team consistently named schedules, supplies, equipment, and sometimes top-down decisions as areas for improvement, but no one suggested Violet change her style. Nor did they reference their working relationships with each other.

Pondering this overnight, Violet woke the next morning with the missing piece. Whereas she used the SI 5 questions that are presented in this book, she relied far too heavily on her employees' first answers and did little to probe for more information. In fact, she recalled, her goal was to limit each stay interview to twenty minutes and proceeded with confidence that her team would open up their innermost thoughts without her coaxing. Then she realized another shortcoming in her approach: If she didn't probe deeply they wouldn't ask for things she couldn't provide. She delighted when they talked about supply shortages because she could fix that with one signature.

But why, then, did Buster really leave? She didn't believe the two excuses he gave and she began to wonder if new equipment was his foremost need when they'd had their stay interview day. Had he held something back?

Three weeks later Violet walked into a coffee shop and saw Buster seated in a back corner, sipping a drink and reading his tablet. Buster was facing away from the line and Violet could have easily bought her coffee and gone on her way. But instead she decided to approach him. With coffee in hand, Violet walked down the aisle and circled around the end to become visible to Buster. He greeted her hesitantly and returned quickly to his screen. With courage up, Violet asked if she could join him and subsequently took a seat across from Buster.

With the air too tense for small talk, Violet got right to it. "Buster, I had no idea you were looking and I want to know why. You never gave one indication you wanted to work somewhere else. I relied on you to be upfront with me and you let me down." Then she softened just a tad and said, "You have no reason to hold back the truth now. Please tell it to me."

Too startled to clear his throat, Buster was caught between saying what he wanted to say and avoiding confrontation, which he preferred. But after looking out the window to his right he turned back to say this: "You know in those stay interviews when you asked what you could do to make our jobs better? You need to go back and ask that question again. But this time ask it like you mean it because it's very hard for people who work for you to be upfront. We just didn't think you'd listen to feedback about you without punishing us for it later."

As those words traveled toward their target, Buster grabbed his drink and tablet and scooted for the door.

The next day Violet sat at her desk and dwelled on what Buster had said, just as she had throughout the sleepless night before. At first she denied his message, thinking it was only Buster who didn't trust her. But her conscience nagged her to dig into the truth. Violet decided then to schedule "stay interview updates" with her direct reports, ostensibly to follow up on stay plan items but really to courageously ask each employee if she did the right behaviors to build their trust.

Five "update" meetings later, Violet had captured the information she needed to know. Scott from Med-Surg told her she listened half-heartedly when he had important things to say, and she therefore dropped the ball on important commitments that resulted from those discussions. Margaret from Emergency disclosed a related but different complaint, that Violet tended to tell the CEO about innovative ideas from her nursing team but kept the spotlight on herself by not disclosing the names of those who came up with the ideas. Edna from Maternity said she had given examples of ideas that would make her job easier but that Violet had presented them mildly to the CEO and ultimately abandoned them rather than take a stronger stand.

The managers for Intensive Care and Oncology squirmed when Violet asked specific relationship questions but she left believing that they had their own stories, too. While the examples she heard along with the frustrated voice tones repulsed her, Violet immediately recognized why her team was suddenly more brazen than just three months ago. Buster had left and maybe now they felt empowered to leave, too. Violet's time to retain her team was short.

Few managers can do the 180-degree style reversal that Violet began that day. With her career on the line, she opened up to the

CEO and asked for feedback and also for a professional coach. She asked her HR executive to advise her on how to take negative feedback nondefensively, and they practiced doing so after hours in her office. She studied her calendar and reconsidered her values for the fifty hours she worked each week. Ultimately, she realized that her success was tied 100 percent to the success of her six direct reports, and that nothing must come before her building and preserving those six relationships based on the bedrock of trust.

Within thirty days Violet again visited with each of her direct reports, asked some hard questions about her own behaviors, and committed to specific positive changes. She would meet with them individually more often, do so with zero distractions, take diligent notes, fulfill her commitments, ensure that the CEO and other executives knew of the employees' own individual accomplishments, back them on tough issues when she agreed they were right . . . and more.

With trust issues addressed, Violet could then focus on real stay interview issues because her team disclosed them openly to her. As a result problems were solved, skill plans were put into place, and relationship issues were confronted when necessary rather than the earlier emphasis on "things." Margaret from Emergency soon told Violet she would retire early, within the next year, so together they identified an internal replacement and built her skills for the job. The next year Scott from Med-Surg answered a call from a head-hunter who dangled a chief nursing job in a neighboring state. Scott immediately told Violet and together they crafted a plan for him to stay. And with so many lessons learned, Violet then asked her team to conduct stay interviews downward with their teams and cautioned them on the greatest lesson of all: Your team will only tell you the truth if they trust you.

❭ ❭ ❭

For sure, this story begins by sounding real and then morphs into a fairy tale. I included it here in this final chapter, though, to make the most compelling point. Not only does the success of stay interviews hinge on trust, but every behavior you do adds to or subtracts from whether your employees trust you. During this book I've written about stay interviews' mechanical aspects, the tactics for preparing for the meeting, starting the meeting, managing the meeting from beginning to end, developing stay plans, conducting forecasts, concluding the meeting effectively, and avoiding the stay interview traps. All of this, though, falls flat without your employees believing in their hearts that they can tell you what they think and you will act on it honorably.

When speaking to groups of CEOs, I ask them to raise their hands if they can think of at least one manager in their companies who has trouble building trust. You can accurately predict that nearly all raise their hands. This moment is important because until then many CEOs have seen trust-building or trust-breaking as the equivalent of any other manager skill, like giving performance feedback or providing career coaching. But then they connect the dots to see that great managers do indeed build trust and those who do not are very, very far from being great. And this applies to first-line supervisors up to those CEOs themselves.

The time has come to close this book and take away its strongest lesson, which is that *no one on your team will tell you anything important if they don't trust you.* So go now to conduct stay interviews with your team to make your career more fruitful and add happiness to your life. Good luck!

# INDEX

CPSIA information can be obtained
at www.ICGtesting.com
Printed in the USA
LVHW04s1135280718
585238LV00002B/26/P